As one of the world's longest established and best-known travel brands, Thomas Cook are the experts in travel.

For more than 135 years our guidebooks have unlocked the secrets of destinations around the world, sharing with travellers a wealth of experience and a passion for travel.

Rely on Thomas Cook as your travelling companion on your next trip and benefit from our unique heritage.

Thomas Cook **traveller** guides

KENYA
Melissa Shales

Your travelling companion since 1873

Thomas
Cook

Written by Melissa Shales, updated by Lisa Voormeij
Original photography by David Watson

Published by Thomas Cook Publishing
A division of Thomas Cook Tour Operations Limited.
Company Registration no. 3772199 England
The Thomas Cook Business Park, Unit 9, Coningsby Road,
Peterborough PE3 8SB, United Kingdom
Email: books@thomascook.com, Tel: + 44 (0) 1733 416477
www.thomascookpublishing.com

Produced by Cambridge Publishing Management Limited
Burr Elm Court, Main Street, Caldecote CB23 7NU

ISBN: 978-1-84848-242-5

© 2003, 2006, 2008 Thomas Cook Publishing
This fourth edition © 2010
Text © Thomas Cook Publishing
Maps © Thomas Cook Publishing/PCGraphics (UK) Limited

Series Editor: Adam Royal
Production/DTP: Steven Collins

Printed and bound in Italy by Printer Trento

Cover photography: Edmund Nagele, Pictures Colour Library

Contents

Introduction

Kenya straddles the equator at the crossroads of Africa, separating the burning deserts of the north from the vast rolling plateaux of the south, its culture built by immigrants from all over Africa, the Middle East, Asia and Europe. Home to one of the world's last great reservoirs of wildlife, it has an extraordinary variety of natural habitats, from coral reefs to open grasslands and tropical forest. Its people live in thatched huts and cosmopolitan cities. Above all, it is quite spectacularly beautiful.

The vast Rift Valley, which slashes its way across the country, is now recognised as the birthplace of mankind. This is the original Garden of Eden. But as in the ancient story, paradise is not without its troubles. Kenya is struggling to survive against drought, a massive population explosion, economic chaos and corruption. The very survival of the country's natural riches depends, to a large extent, on tourism. Over the years, Kenya has developed one of the most sophisticated tourist infrastructures on the continent. Every option is available – from a lazy fortnight under the coconut palms to high adventure out in the bush, far away from civilisation, from tiny tents to luxury hotels that rival the finest in the world.

With a temperate climate and such a diverse landscape and culture, most people travel to this part of East Africa for the safaris, and Kenya has some of the top game reserves and national parks on the continent. Plenty of other activities are on offer in Kenya, too, including trekking the glacial ridges of Mount Kenya, exploring the Chalbi Desert on camels or scuba diving at Malindi Marine National Park on the Indian Ocean coast. Kenyan culture, too, is fascinating, particularly the traditional nomadic lifestyles of the Maasai and Samburu tribes.

Kenya's natural beauty is idyllic, though the land and its people often suffer from droughts, tribal conflicts and political instability. At the end of 2007 and in early 2008 Kenya experienced violence following the disputed presidential election between two opposing party leaders, and in 2009 the country endured yet another drought, affecting the lives of thousands of Kenyans and much of the wildlife. At the time of writing, political tension between tribes in Kenya remains. Although tourism is rarely affected, it is advisable to check with your Foreign Ministry or State Department before travelling to Kenya.

Kenya

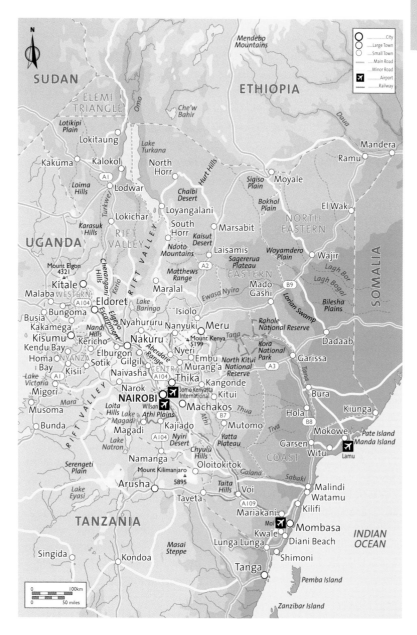

The land

Kenya is a country put together by the British at the end of the 19th century from a network of tribal territories. The total area of 582,750sq km (225,000sq miles), with altitudes ranging from sea level to 5,199m (17,057ft), is split roughly in half by the equator, and includes every conceivable sort of terrain from snow-capped volcanoes to arid desert, as well as the coastline. About 2 per cent of the country is made up of water, the majority of this being in the massive lakes, Victoria and Turkana. Of its eight main rivers, the longest is the Tana at 700km (435 miles).

Geology

The oldest known rocks in Kenya, dating back about 3,000 million years, are found in the plains of the south and west (Lake Victoria, the Masai Mara and Tsavo). About 1,000 million years ago volcanic activity formed sheets of lava and intrusions of gold-bearing granite and quartz, as well as the softer rhyolites, mined today as Kisii soapstone.

About 500 million years ago the land buckled, creating a vast mountain range stretching nearly 6,000km (3,728 miles) from the Middle East to Mozambique. This is the basis for Kenya's Central Highlands.

THOMAS COOK'S KENYA

Almost as soon as the country was opened up, Thomas Cook was taking parties down the Nile and through the Sudan. Most of their tours were hunting safaris centred on Nairobi. Then a local manager set up the first motoring tour of East Africa in 1935, which became the prototype for all motoring safaris today.

Great rivers sprang up, wending their way across the ancient plains to the sea. As the mountains eroded, these rivers carried the sediments downstream and, from 300 million years ago onwards, laid them out across the coastal plains. From about 180 to 70 million years ago (the heyday of the dinosaurs), this plain was invaded by the sea, which stretched far inland to where Mount Kenya now stands.

The next dramatic shift began about 70 million years ago as two parallel stretches of the largely eroded mountains began to bulge upwards, creating new ranges separated by a shallow depression. Twenty million years ago this valley began to split in a series of earthquakes and volcanic eruptions which created the Rift Valley (*see pp54–61*). Since then, intense volcanic activity has continued in and around the Rift, throwing up all Kenya's greatest mountains, from Mount Kenya to the crater volcanoes, such as Longonot.

Most are now extinct, but there is still considerable activity under the surface. Mount Teleki, near Lake Turkana, last erupted in 1899, while the crater of Central Island, Lake Turkana, was billowing ash in the 1960s.

Numerous hot springs are found along the Rift Valley, and those just to the south of Lake Naivasha have been harnessed at the Olkaria geothermal power station.

Natural resources

Despite all this geological upheaval, Kenya has relatively few mineral resources. There are deposits of gold, silver, iron and lead, but the amounts are too small for profitable exploitation. Soda is mined at Lake Magadi, and there is some mining for gemstones such as garnet, but it is the fossils – coral, limestone and diatomite – that have proved to be the most lucrative minerals. By far, Kenya's greatest resources, however, are its fertile agricultural lands, and the wildlife and coast which bring in tourism.

The economy

Kenya has a wide manufacturing base, mainly for home consumption, although some of the produce spills over into neighbouring African countries. It also acts as a trading centre for Central and East Africa, controlling much of the region's shipping and fuel distribution.

Tourism has recently become the country's greatest earner of foreign exchange, but agriculture is still the bedrock of the economy, with some 76 per cent of the population living off the land. The main cash crops are coffee and tea, sisal, pyrethrum and pineapples, and, to a lesser extent, other fruit, cotton, tobacco and sugar cane. One sees expanses of polytunnels for flower cultivation, especially near Naivasha. Flowers now make up 8 per cent of Kenya's exports.

A carpet of tea across the Kericho Hills in western Kenya

The land

FLORA

Bright, wonderful and often weird, Kenya's flora is extraordinarily diverse, with some 10,000 species catalogued, from tiny wayside flowers to giant hardwood trees. For most casual visitors, however, the floral landscape, as it exists today, is strongly influenced by man. Away from wildlife and wilderness areas, few of the most spectacular flowering plants and trees, and nearly all the agricultural crops, are indigenous.

Kenya has a wide range of indigenous euphorbias, from tiny shrubs to trees

Garden Kenya

Indigenous Kenyans are rarely interested in flower gardens, preferring to use the land for more practical purposes, but Kenya still has some wonderful gardens.

In the mid-19th century, the British ruled half the world and traded with the other half. They were also obsessive gardeners and today, one of the easiest ways of tracing their presence is by the fantastic variety of flowering plants they swapped across the globe. Urban roads were planted with trees to create superb avenues of purple jacaranda (from South America) or scarlet flame trees (from Madagascar). Garden fences are incandescent with sweeping bougainvillaea (from Brazil). From the Americas also come the bright cascades of golden shower, poinsettias, big as trees, with bracts of scarlet, pink, yellow and white, and the creamy white and yellow flowers of the frangipani. From China they imported the hibiscus bush,

with its glossy leaves and huge, brilliantly coloured flowers, and from Europe they brought roses and daisies, to remind them of home.

Agricultural Kenya

The coconut floated over from Polynesia thousands of years ago, and some crops, sorghum and gourds, for instance, are indigenous. But the agricultural landscape of today is a largely modern European creation. Crops range from maize, potatoes and wheat to citrus (from China), tea and coffee. Many of the working forests are now planted with quick-growing imports such as eucalyptus, originally brought in from Australia to produce firewood, and pine.

Indigenous plants

Kenya's indigenous species grow in a series of clearly defined altitude bands.

At the lowest levels, one of the most interesting trees is the vast, fleshy baobab, said to have angered the gods and been planted upside-down, and the dense, twisted mangrove that lines some areas of the coast, growing through the silt and salty water. Between 1,000 and 1,500m (3,300–4,900ft), the prevailing vegetation is coarse savannah grass with some 40 different species of acacia, from small, scrubby thorn bushes to the huge yellow fever tree made famous in Rudyard Kipling's *Just So Stories*. Amid the grasses hide several species of convolvulus, aloes and a range of euphorbias from ground-hugging creepers to the cactus-like candelabra tree. These are all tough plants that have evolved protective features that enable them to survive the burning equatorial sun and the long periods of drought that ravage the land.

The forests start at about 1,500m (4,900ft), although little remains at lower levels. Not only is this the prime agricultural belt, but also where most of the great slow-growing hardwoods, such as mahogany, teak and ebony once thrived; now most have been felled for timber. To find large expanses of intact forest, you have to climb above 2,500m (8,200ft), into the impenetrable tangle of cedar, hagenia and bamboo. This is a shadowy, green world where tiny orchids hide in knotted tree trunks, thick lianas hang like rope, flowering creepers provide sudden splashes of bright colour, and grey Spanish moss drips like ancient cobwebs from the leaves.

At 3,000m (9,800ft), the forest ends abruptly and you come out on to open heath, where red-hot pokers, gladioli and delphiniums splash the land with colour. But these dazzling plants just form a backdrop for Africa's giant alpine species – tree heather, giant groundsel and great plumes of lobelia, 9m (29¹/₂ft) high. Surely these are the most wonderful plants of all.

Cascades of bougainvillaea turn gardens technicolour

FAUNA
Birds

The big mammals may be the main draw to the Kenyan countryside, but in terms of variety and sheer numbers, they pale into insignificance against the country's feathered population. Kenya has over 1,000 known species of birds. More are still being discovered, and even the most humble nature trail can sometimes provide the dedicated twitcher with sightings of up to 50 different species. Kenya's birds range in size from the tiny sunbird to the huge ostrich, and cover every colour of the rainbow and a few more besides.

Open savannah and woodland

Of all Kenya's birds, the 2m (6½ft) tall ostrich is king, roaming the open grasslands in small family groups. The males are black with white tail feathers, the females a dusty brown. In spite of having wings, these large birds are flightless, their body weight too great for them to lift off the ground. To compensate, they have evolved into very fast runners with a powerful kick.

Other birds to watch out for in open country include ground-living guineafowl and francolins and tree- and ground-dwelling hornbills, with their huge, hooked bills. Tiny, jewel-like sunbirds hover above the bushes; trees hang heavy with the nests of golden and crimson weaver birds. Around the lodges cluster sociable wood-hoopoes, flocks of brightly coloured waxbills, iridescent blue/black glossy starlings

Yellow-billed stork in the coastal mangrove swamps near Watamu

and brilliant, superb starlings with green backs, russet chests, white collars and turquoise heads.

Birds of prey and scavengers

There are six species of vulture found in Kenya, of which the most common is the white-backed vulture with a 2.3m (7½ft) wingspan. Scavengers of carrion, these large, ungainly birds with hunched backs and bald heads wheel around the sky, perch on high branches, or scrabble round a kill, their heads dripping in blood. Another common scavenger is the Marabou stork, nearly 2m (6½ft) tall, with a grey back, white front and ruff and a bald, pink head.

There are numerous different birds of prey, including harriers, goshawks, sparrowhawks, buzzards, kites, falcons, kestrels and eagles. Look out in particular for the African fish eagle, a black, white and chestnut giant that lives near fresh water and has a haunting scream, and the huge, tawny, Martial Eagle, with white, spotted legs, stunning for its sheer size. The leggy, crested Secretarybird, which gains its name from the similarity of its features to black trousers, grey jacket and the quill pen-like feathers stuck behind its ear, stalks the grassland, preying on insects and reptiles, including small snakes.

Waterbirds

The greatest concentrations of birdlife are to be found along the line of the Rift Valley. Some of the best freshwater birdwatching is at Lake Baringo, where herons, cranes, cormorants, darters and storks perch on the rocky shoreline, eyeing their prey; several species of kingfishers dart through the shadows; ducks, geese and moorhens bob across the ripples; and plovers, ibis and sandpipers stalk the shallows.

The alkaline soda lakes, such as Bogoria or Nakuru, provide a whole new set of birds. One of the greatest sights the country has to offer is the massive sheets of thousands of pink flamingoes carpeting the shallow lakes, while clouds of pelicans skim the surface of the water.

This round-up only covers the tiniest fragment of Kenya's teeming birdlife. A good guide for those interested in learning more is *The Birds of Kenya and Northern Tanzania* by Zimmerman, Turner and Pearson. If you plan to do any serious birdwatching, you will also need a good pair of binoculars. Many

An ostrich family out for a stroll in Meru National Park

of the lodges and hotels in the best bird watching areas will provide lists of species seen on locally guided walks with ornithologists. Some tour companies (*see p189*) will even run birdwatching safaris.

Mammals

Kenya boasts some 300 species of mammals. It is obviously impossible to describe them all here, so this list concentrates on the more common and visible species. Those who wish to know more should refer to the *Collins Field Guide to the Larger Mammals of Africa*.

Bushbuck *Tragelaphus scriptus*

A smallish antelope (80cm/31in at the shoulder), the bushbuck's rump is higher than the shoulders, giving it a hunched appearance. It has white patches on the neck and white spots on the flanks. Males have slightly twisted, 30cm (12in) long horns.

OTHER ANTELOPE TO LOOK OUT FOR

Bongo: chestnut with white stripes and long horns up to 1.2m (47in) tall. Rare, timid and nocturnal, living in high montane forest.

Duiker: fawny grey, up to 60cm (24in) tall. There are four species in Kenya. Though common, they are rarely seen as they are nocturnal and live in dense woodland and long grass.

Roan antelope: the size of a horse, uniformly tan, with a black and white face and swept-back ridged horns. Rare in Kenya, found in the Lambwe Valley and Shimba Hills.

Sable antelope: a glossy black giant with huge sickle-shaped horns, white underparts and stripy face. Found only in the Shimba Hills.

Sitatunga: like a shaggy, darker bushbuck in appearance. Very rare; found only at Lake Victoria, Saiwa Swamp and Lewa.

There are 40 different subspecies, ranging in colour from light chestnut with white stripes to a dull greyish brown. Mainly nocturnal, they live alone in well-watered woodland across the country.

The huge, elegant sable antelope is rare in Kenya, found only in the Shimba Hills

Dik-dik *Rhynchotragus kirki/guentheri*
There are two species in Kenya, both minute and dainty (30–40cm/12–16in high and weighing 3–5kg/6½–11lb), with a greyish brown coat and tiny, straight horns (males only). Guenther's are slightly smaller than Kirk's. Usually seen in pairs, they live in savannah and scrub.

Eland *Taurotragus oryx*
Huge (2m/6½ft at the shoulder) with a tawny, cow-like body, a dewlap at the neck, faint white stripes across the back and black hair along the spine and under the belly. Males and females have long, backward-lying horns with a tight spiral at the base. They live in large herds in open savannah, mainly in the Samburu region.

Gerenuk *Litocranius walleri*
A smallish gazelle (80cm/31in at the shoulder) with a russet back, tawny sides and white underbelly. It has white rings and black tear-drops around the eyes and is known as 'giraffe-necked' because of its elongated neck. Males have curved, ringed horns. They live alone or in small groups in the dry northern scrub and stand on their hind legs to feed.

Grant's gazelle *Gazella granti*
A medium-sized gazelle (up to 90cm/ 35in at the shoulders), with a tawny back, slightly darker stripe along the flanks and white underbelly. It has a white patch, outlined in black, around

The gentle and gregarious impala, in Tsavo West National Park

the tail. The face has whitish stripes from eye to nose. Males and females have long, ridged, bent horns. They live in small herds in savannah and dry scrubland throughout Kenya.

Hartebeest *Alcelaphus buselaphus*
A large, distinctive antelope (1.5m/60in at the shoulder), with a uniform tan coat and steeply sloping back. It has a very long narrow face and thick, ridged horns shaped like a candelabrum. They live in large herds in open grassland and are widely distributed across Kenya.

Impala *Aepyceros melampus*
A medium-sized gazelle (90cm/35in at the shoulder), they have a russet back, paler sides and a white underbelly. They have black stripes on the tail and rump and the face is tawny with a darker strip

Baboon mother and baby

along the nose. The males have long, lyre-shaped horns. They live in large herds on the edge of woodland and are found in most areas of the country. Renowned athletes, they can jump heights of up to 3m (10ft) and have recorded speeds of 96kp/h (60mph).

Klipspringer *Oreotragus oreotragus*
Small (50cm/20in at the shoulder), with a long, bristly coat of speckled yellowish grey and whitish underbelly. The triangular face has black and white rings around the eyes and large, black-rimmed ears. Males have short, ridged horns. They seem to walk on tiptoe, are agile climbers, and live in rocky areas in small groups.

Lesser kudu *Tragelaphus imberbis*
Large (1.1m/43in at the shoulder), with a brownish grey coat and up to 15 narrow white stripes across the back. The head is darker with a white chevron between the eyes and two white patches

on the neck. Males have long, loosely spiralling horns. They live in dense acacia scrubland in pairs or small groups, mainly in the southeast. The greater kudu (*Tragelaphus strepsiceros*),

PRIMATES

Vervet monkeys (*Cercopithecus aethiops*) are the smallest of Kenya's four main species of primates. They have brown backs, lighter stomachs and dark faces, and little fear of people; they often hang around hotels.
Olive baboons (*Papio anubis*) are also common, living in large troops in open woodland. They are much bigger, with a yellowy-brown coat and square, dog-like face. They can be dangerous. Much rarer are the monkey species that dwell in the high montane forests.
The **blue monkey** (*Cercopithecus mitis*) is thickset with a dense bluish-grey coat, black legs and black band around the shoulders and long white whiskers around the face.
The most beautiful is the **Abyssinian black-and-white colobus monkey** (*Colobus abyssinicus*), large, jet black, with a white muzzle, white-fringed cape across its back and a long white plume at the end of its tail.

found only at Lake Bogoria, Marsabit and Lewa, is larger (1.5m/59in at the shoulder) with eight to ten white stripes and a beard.

Oribi *Ourebia ourebi*
Small (60cm/24in at the shoulder), with a light chestnut coat, white underbelly, large black-tipped ears and white rings around the eyes. Males have short, spiky horns. They live in small groups in long grass throughout Kenya.

Oryx *Oryx beisa*
Large (1.2m/47in at the shoulder), reddish tan with a white underbelly, black stripes along the spine and flanks and black garters round the front legs. The face is black and white, and both males and females have very long, straight ridged horns. They live in large herds in open scrub in northern Kenya.

Reedbuck
There are two species in Kenya. The Bohor reedbuck (*Redunca redunca*) is small (90cm/35in at the shoulder) with a thick, bright tan coat, white underbelly and chin and paler circles around the eyes. Males have short, stubby, forward-curving horns. They live in pairs in long grass near water throughout Kenya. The less common mountain reedbuck (*Redunca fulvorufula*) has a greyish, woolly coat. It lives in small herds in rocky mountains and scrub.

Thomson's gazelle *Gazella thomsoni*
Small (60cm/24in at the shoulder) with

Oryx grazing in northern scrubland

The reticulated giraffe is recognised by its darker, even patching

a light chestnut coat, white underparts and black stripes along the flanks and on the rump. The face is whitish with a darker streak down the nose and black stripes along the cheeks, and they have fairly long, ridged and slightly curved horns. They live in large, often migratory, herds in open grassland.

Topi *Damaliscus korrigum*
Large (1.3m/51in at the shoulder), with a sleek, dark-chestnut coat, long face and large purplish smudges on the nose, legs and rump. They live in large herds in open grassland, but in Kenya are only found in the Masai Mara.

Waterbuck
The Defassa waterbuck (*Kobus defassa*) is large (1.3m/51in at the shoulder), with a shaggy, dark greyish brown coat,

a white muzzle and white patch under the chin. Its most noticeable feature is a large white patch on the rump. The males have long, ridged, curving horns. The common waterbuck (*Kobus ellipsiprymnus*) has a white circle on its rump. Both live in small herds in open woodland and marsh.

Plains animals
African buffalo *Syncerus caffer*
Huge, ox-like creatures, up to 1.65m (5¹/₂ft) tall at the shoulder, with an almost black coat and short, heavy horns like a viking helmet. They live in a variety of habitats from thick forest, where they stay in small groups, to open grassland where they gather in large herds. Seemingly placid, they can be very bad-tempered if aroused, especially old bulls.

Elephant *Loxodonta africana*
The African elephant is the world's largest land mammal, reaching heights of 3.3m (11ft) at the shoulder, with tusks up to 3m (10ft) long. They live up to 70 years, are highly intelligent and have sophisticated social behaviour. Herds vary from family groups of five or six to hundreds and they adapt to many habitats from open plains to thick forest. One of the elephant's nearest relative is the tiny, rabbit-like rock hyrax.

Giraffe *Giraffa camelopardalis*
Living in herds of up to 70 in open woodland, giraffes are graceful

creatures, measuring up to 6m (20ft) tall, that move with a peculiar rocking-horse gallop. The most common race is the southern Masai giraffe, with a light tan coat and smudgy, irregular brown spots. The rare, western race, Rothschild giraffe has white socks and a more pronounced bump on the forehead, while the males have four horns. The reticulated giraffe is a separate species found in northern Kenya, and has a paler undercoat and crisply defined, dark-red crazy paving.

Hippopotamus *Hippopotamus amphibius*

Up to 1.7m (5½ft) high at the shoulder, hippos have enormous barrel bodies completely out of proportion to their short legs. They spend their days in the water, in sociable huddles, coming out

THE 'BIG FIVE'

The concept of the 'Big Five'– namely, lion, elephant, rhino, buffalo and leopard – is an extremely limiting one. Many superb wildlife viewing safaris may involve none of these animals, so try and look beyond the hype.

to graze at night. Generally placid, they can be dangerous if disturbed. If you see one yawn – a cavernous experience – you can believe the stories of them biting a canoe in half.

Rhinoceros

Now extremely rare, rhinos live alone or in pairs in a variety of habitats from open scrub to dense montane forest. There are two species, the black rhino (*Diceros bicornis*), indigenous to Kenya, and the white rhino (*Ceratotherium* (*Cont. on p20*)

Herd of Burchell's (common) zebra, usually seen in the company of antelope and wildebeest

The golden horn

Since the Greek astronomer Ptolemy first visited the coast in the 2nd century AD, East Africa has been trading in ivory and rhino horn, which was thought by the Chinese to be an aphrodisiac and by the Arabs a symbol of manhood. For centuries, the situation remained stable. But with the arrival of the Europeans all that was to change.

Armed with high-powered hunting rifles, thousands set off on safari, shooting anything that moved. By the 1930s, they were game-spotting from the air and using high-powered rifles. Large bulls, with their huge tusks, were especially sought after.

In 1977, with elephant and rhino numbers at an alarmingly low level, Kenya finally banned their hunting,

An increasingly rare live black rhino

Elephant herd heading towards the Mara River

but the new scarcity of rhino horn and ivory led to soaring prices. At its peak, ivory was worth about US$300 and rhino horn over US$2,000 a kilo. With such glittering prizes at stake, poachers began a wholesale slaughter, using machine guns and helicopters and paying officials to turn a blind eye. A decade on, Kenya had lost nearly two-thirds of its elephants, some 1,500 a year were being shot and rhino stocks were down to a couple of hundred.

In 1989, a worldwide ban on ivory and horn was enforced. Kenya made a massive, dramatic bonfire of confiscated tusks and began to reorganise, giving its rangers military training and equipment and instituting a 'shoot-to-kill' policy. It has been remarkably successful. Prices have plummeted. Elephant numbers are rising in a healthy manner. In Tsavo East and West, there are now over 8,000. However, black rhino numbers are still critical and the species is critically endangered. Presently, there are probably between 500 and 600 black rhinos in Kenya. Most are in highly protected sanctuaries such as Tsavo West's Ngulia, which has about 50 of them, and private reserves such as Lewa and Solio.

Lions on a wildebeest kill

simum), which is imported for restocking from southern Africa. Both are the same colour, but the black is smaller, with a pointed upper lip. White comes from the Afrikaans word *weiss*, meaning wide, and the true name of the species is the square-lipped rhino.

Warthog *Phacochoerus aethiopicus*
A small and intensely ugly bush pig, the warthog has a greyish skin, with a dark mane, an elongated snout with lumpy warts above the eyes and on the cheeks, and small, upward curving tusks. They live in open grassland, in nuclear families, and stick their tails up like flags when they run.

Wildebeest *Connochaetes taurinus*
Technically an antelope, the wildebeest, or brindled gnu, has been described as

having 'the forequarters of an ox, the hindquarters of an antelope and the tail of a horse'. Measuring up to 1.5m (5ft) at the shoulder, they have a greyish brown coat, huge, dark head with a straggly mane and beard, and small, thick horns that meet across the forehead. They gather in vast herds for the migration (*see also p80*).

Zebra
There are two species of these black and white striped wild horses in Kenya. The more common is Burchell's zebra (*Equus [Hippotigris] burchelli*), with broad, uneven striping. Grevy's zebra (*Equus [Dolichohippus] grevyi*) is found only in Laikipia. It has many thin stripes, a white belly and large donkey-like ears. Only Burchell's zebra take part in Serengeti-type migrations.

Predators

Cheetah *Acinonyx jubatus*

Tawny, with round, black spots and a small, neat head with black stripes round the muzzle, the cheetah is sleek and elegant, built for speed. They have clocked record-breaking speeds of up to 112kp/h over 400m (70mph over ¹/₄ mile). They live alone or in mother–sibling groups in open savannah and hunt usually in the early morning.

Jackal

Small, fox-like animals that survive by scavenging and hunting small animals. Largely nocturnal, they usually live in pairs in open savannah. There are three species in Kenya, all with brown to yellowish grey coats: the golden jackal (*Canis aureus*); the side-striped (*Canis adustus*) with a white stripe along the flanks; and the black-backed (*Canis mesomelas*).

Leopard *Panthera pardus*

Long, low and immensely powerful, the leopard has clustered rings of dark spots on a rich red-gold background. Living solitary lives in rocky hills and woodland, they are nocturnal hunters, rarely seen in the daytime, which they spend hiding in caves or high branches.

Lion *Panthera leo*

The largest of the great cats of Africa, lions can reach up to 90cm/35in in height at the shoulder and have a uniform tawny coloured coat. Only the males have manes. They usually live in prides of up to 30 animals in open savannah. Males make a lot of noise, but the females do all the work, hunting at night, or dawn.

Spotted hyena *Crocuta crocuta*

A large, dog-like animal with powerful head and shoulders, a steeply sloping back and weak back legs, the hyena has a scruffy, tawny coat with blackish spots. Efficient scavengers, they also prey on a wide range of animals. They generally live in small packs, but gather in large groups before mating and sometimes set up nurseries for the young. Largely nocturnal, they have a range of distinctive cries, from piercing howls to a terrifyingly eerie laugh.

A cheetah surveys its domain

The land

History

4–2 million years ago	Excavations provide the earliest known evidence of human existence on earth, suggesting the East African Rift Valley as the birthplace of mankind.
200,000–150,000 BC	The Rift Valley is home to Acheulian Stone Age cultures.
10,000–5000 BC	Hunter-gatherer tribes, related to the San and Khoikhoi of South Africa, live in Kenya.
2000–1000 BC	Cushite migrations south from Ethiopia and Somalia (*see p28*).
1000 BC	Earliest Nilotic migration from the Nile Valley.
500 BC–AD 500	Earliest Bantu migration from West Africa. Readjustment of tribal boundaries continues until frozen by the British in the 19th century.
650–800	Arab and Persian trading posts are set up along the coast. Traders settle and intermarry, introducing the Islamic religion and creating the Swahili people and language.

1498–99	Portuguese explorer Vasco da Gama sets up a trading post at Malindi.
Early 16th century	Mombasa sacked twice by the Portuguese, who take over as rulers.
1696–98	Portuguese settlements attacked and conquered by Omanis.
1741	Mazrui governor of Mombasa declares independence from Oman.
1824	The Mazrui sign a treaty offering a loose British Protectorate.
1826–37	British aid withdrawn and the Mazrui are defeated. Sultan of Oman moves his capital to Zanzibar.
1873	Omani-British treaty bans the export of slaves and closes all slave markets.
1895	British Government declares East Africa a Protectorate, taking over direct rule.
1896–1901	East African Railway opens up the Kenya highlands.

1907	Nairobi becomes capital of East African Protectorate.
1920–23	The East African Protectorate becomes a Crown Colony. Cheap land offered to British ex-servicemen, leading to large-scale immigration.
1950–60	Mau Mau terror campaign by Kikuyu nationalists seeking independence. In total, 13,500 Africans and 100 Europeans die.
1963	Independence, with Jomo Kenyatta as prime minister.
1964	Kenya becomes a republic, with Kenyatta as executive president.
1968	A policy of Africanisation is instated. Land bought from white settlers is given to African farmers. Large-scale emigration by Asians.
1974	Kiswahili becomes the official language.
1978	Kenyatta dies. Vice-President Daniel Arap Moi succeeds him without elections.
1987	Kenya declared a one-party state under the Kenya African National Union.
1992	International pressure forces President Moi to hold elections. Half a million refugees arrive from war-torn Somalia.
1997	Elections held; Moi and his KANU party win, allegedly through rigging.
1998	Terrorists bomb US embassy in Nairobi.
2002	On Dec 30th, Mwai Kibaki becomes Kenya's third president.
2007	Kibaki returned in suspect elections. Over 1,000 people killed in protest riots.
2008	A period of instability and violence follows the disputed elections, but by April 2008 a power-sharing agreement is reached. Kibaki remains as president, with his rival Raila Odinga, of the Orange Democratic Movement, as prime minister.
2010	Although the government has stabilised, political tension remains and the people of Kenya are literally arming themselves in anticipation of the upcoming 2012 elections.

Politics

Kenya is a Commonwealth Republic. It has a single house of parliament of 200 members, 188 elected by universal suffrage, and 12 appointed by the president, who governs with the aid of a 33-member cabinet. Now, as at independence, the country is officially a multi-party democracy, but the road between has been rocky.

Kenyatta's rule

The 1963 elections were contested by two parties, the Kenya African National Union (KANU) and the Kenya African Democratic Union (KADU), both splinters of the Kikuyu Kenya African Union (KAU). In 1964 they merged, and Kenya became an unofficial one-party state. During Kenyatta's presidency, however, this did not seem oppressive. Kenya was a beacon of wealth and stability compared with many black African countries.

Moi's rule

In 1978, however, Kenyatta died and was succeeded by his vice-president, Daniel Arap Moi. From the first, criticism was silenced and after the failed Air Force coup in 1982, all opposition was stifled. In 1987, the country officially became a one-party state, the press was muzzled and Moi's powers were increased.

In 1992, international pressure forced Moi to hold multi-party elections with a secret ballot, monitored by international observers. Two main opposition parties, the Democratic Party and FORD, the Forum for the Restoration of Democracy, were created, divided along tribal lines. The Kikuyu switched their allegiance to the DP, while FORD was

Kenya's Parliament Building in Nairobi

Politics

KENYATTA

Johnstone Kamau was born c.1892, son of a Kikuyu peasant. Educated at a local mission, he changed his name to Jomo Kenyatta and moved to Nairobi where he became deeply involved in politics. From 1931, he spent 15 years in London, returning to Kenya as the acknowledged leader of the nationalist movement in 1946. In 1953 he was arrested as a suspected Mau Mau leader, and spent the next seven years in prison. On his release in 1961, he won the country's first elections as leader of KANU, and at independence, in 1963, he became prime minister. The following year, he was made president, a position he held until his death in 1978. Known as Mzee (Father or Elder), he was not only the Father of the Kenyan nation, but one of the great heroes of African nationalism, and a distinguished and respected world leader.

largely supported by the Luo. Campaigning was based on personality and dirt-mongering. Policies were hardly mentioned. Inter-tribal violence broke out, and politicians openly handed out sackfuls of money. By the time of the election, the opposition was hopelessly fragmented, with seven presidential candidates.

In the end, Moi and KANU stayed in power, but now they only had a narrow majority in Parliament. During the 1990s and into the new millennium, in spite of general freedom of speech, Kenya continued with a relatively repressive constitution, with all the power in the hands of the president. The economy was in crisis and, with the emergence of other holiday destinations, especially in southern Africa, the tourist business started to falter.

By 2002, Kenya was in crisis on a number of fronts. Most critical was the issue of corruption, so serious that the IMF, the World Bank and members of the EU began to refuse further aid to Kenya unless it cleaned up its act. Added to this, the economy was in free-fall, and AIDS was beginning to reduce Kenyans' life expectancy drastically.

Kibaki's rule

There was great hope for improvement when Mwai Kibaki became Kenya's third president in December 2002. However, any changes were mainly cosmetic and serious corruption in government continued. This was typified by the clearly rigged elections in December 2007, when Kibaki was returned for a second term. Opposition supporters rioted, over 1,000 people were killed and more than 300,000 were left homeless. The former UN Secretary-General, Kofi Annan, managed to broker a peace deal in early 2008, persuading Kibaki to agree to a form of power sharing with his opponent, Raila Odinga.

Power-sharing agreements were finalised in April 2008 as Kibaki, remaining as President, named a Grand Coalition cabinet of 40 ministers, while Odinga was sworn in as prime minister. Tension between tribes in Kenya remains, however – predominantly in the Rift Valley and Central Province. There is unease over what will happen during the upcoming 2012 elections.

Culture

Kenya has few architectural masterpieces and little visual/physical history. Until a century ago, there was no written language. Nevertheless, the country has one of the most complex and fascinating cultures in the world, with the population of about 40 million made up of some 40 different tribes. Since the 7th century, the region has traded with Arabs, Persians and Chinese, all of whom left their mark on the culture, while the arrival of the British Empire turned the whole country on its head.

In spite of this diversity, the tribes share many characteristics so completely different from western culture that new arrivals in the country, ranging from colonial settlers to IMF inspectors, have all found it difficult to understand.

Land and wealth
The idea of money was first introduced by the British. Before that, coastal traders bartered, while the pastoral tribes kept their wealth in cattle and used sheep and goats as day-to-day currency. Hard cash has taken over now, but few of the herders are willing to relinquish their animals altogether.

Among the cultivators, land is also crucial. Most tribes had strict laws of ownership and inheritance long before the Europeans came. Today, even town dwellers usually have a small garden plot or *shamba* in the country, farmed for them by their wives or families. As the population explodes, attempts to find new land to colonise are creating a whole new set of tribal confrontations.

Loyalties and leadership
Few people ever say they are Kenyans first and foremost; their identity comes from their tribe, and their loyalty belongs, above all, to their wives and children and to brothers and sisters by the same mother. After that comes a duty to siblings by other mothers (many people are still polygamous), to the extended family, and finally, to clan and tribe. Europeans may fume about nepotism and lack of patriotism, but the concept of country is almost totally irrelevant, and it is considered only proper that a man in authority help his kinsfolk first.

The tribal elders and chiefs act as judge and jury, intermediary and guide. Their word is law and they are treated with enormous respect. This gives a status to old people lost in Western society, but simultaneously, it also undermines the Western view of democracy. Few dare question the decisions or actions of this supreme council and many will still vote according to the dictates of their chief.

Religion

The Maasai believe in the god 'Enkai' who chose them above all tribes and gave them all the cattle in the world. Somalis who live near the coast are Muslim. Elsewhere, rival bands of missionaries have made Christianity a growth industry, as many people combine aspects of traditional religions with Christianity.

It is easily done. Many of the traditional religions believed in one god, while they used ancestors in the same way that Catholics use saints, as conduits to God and guardians of the living. There is still a profound belief in magic and the local 'witchdoctor' will be consulted about curses while physical ailments are handed over to Western medicine.

Traditionally, in some tribes, both men and women must be circumcised, unless they are prepared to leave the tribe or remain unmarried.

The role of women

Kenyan women, from all tribes, carry the vast majority of the workload. In addition to running the home and family, doing all the cooking and cleaning, fetching of water and firewood, they will do at least some of the farming and are often also responsible for physically building their house. They are respected within the home, but traditionally have no say in public affairs. If a woman returns, or is sent back, to her family, her husband may remarry, but she is unlikely to and will get no further support either for herself or her children. Few women have the opportunity for any but the most basic education and only a

Fisherman in a dugout canoe, off the Mombasa coast

handful have made it on to the first rung of the career ladder. In other African countries socialism has provided sexual equality as a goal, if not a reality. In Kenya, many women find this an elusive concept, although it is not completely alien.

The tribes of Kenya

In Kenya, tribal identity is all-important. There are some 40 different tribes in the country, made up of three main groupings. The Cushites began arriving from Ethiopia and Somalia in about 2000 BC and are still heading south in sporadic waves. The Nilotic tribes came down from Egypt and the Sudan from about 1000 BC, while the Bantu are later migrants, drifting over from West Africa since about 500 BC.

The original hunter-gatherers who lived here prior to 2000 BC were killed, pushed out or absorbed by intermarriage and no longer have any separate identity. The groupings are almost purely linguistic, and among the many tribes who share common roots, you can find every type of lifestyle from hunter-gatherers to nomadic herders, settled farmers and fishermen.

There are no accurate census statistics, but three tribes, the Kikuyu, the Luyia and the Luo, together make up over half of the population. Other tribes range from the Kipsigis, at 3 million, to the tiny El Molo, the smallest tribe in Kenya with about 500 members (*see p132*).

The Bantu

The Bantu tribes are industrious farmers who have become the largest and wealthiest of the three tribal groups. The Kikuyu alone number nearly 7 million (*see pp70–71*). The majority – the Kikuyu, Embu, Meru, Mbeeri, Kamba and Tharaka – live in the Central Highlands. The Mijikenda group of nine sub-tribes (including the Giriama) lives in the coastal hinterland, while the Pokomo group of 13 sub-tribes inhabits the Tana River area. In the west are the Gusii, Suba, Kuria and the Luyia group of 17 sub-tribes.

The Cushites

The Cushites make up a tiny fragment of Kenya's population, clinging to survival on the fringes of habitable country in the northern deserts, the desolate Turkana area and the coastal hinterland. Among the many tribes, only the Somali number more than a few thousand. Others include the Boran, Burji, Dassenich, Gabbra, Orma, Sakuye, Boni, Wata, Yaaka, Dahalo, Galla, Rendille and El Molo.

The Nilotic tribes

There are three main sub-groups within the Nilotic tribes. One is made up of the nomadic herders – the Maasai, who spread across the south of the country, the Samburu who occupy the centre, and the Turkana in the northwest (*see pp129 & 132*). Romantic and decorative figures, fewer than a million all told, they are the most famous

Culture

Luo fisherman mending his nets beside Lake Victoria

people of Kenya and the most reluctant to embrace Western culture.

Next comes a series of tiny tribes – the Kipsigis, Nandi, Tugen, Marakwet, Keiyo, Pokot, Terik and Sabaot – known collectively as the Kalenjin. Settled farmers, many of them live in the Rift Valley area. Under former president Moi, a Tugen, the Kalenjin have become a powerful political force.

Finally, in the far west, around the shores of Lake Victoria, are the farming and fishing Luo, with a population of 4.2 million, the second largest tribe in Kenya. Prime minister Raila Odinga is a Luo.

More recent developments

The situation is still changing although tension remains. The Swahili culture is a mix of the coastal Bantu peoples and various Arab groups (*see pp122–3*). There has been constant movement south from Somalia, from the violent intrusions of the Galla in the 16th century to the flood of over half a million refugees in the last few years. Intermarriage has blurred both territorial boundaries and physiological features.

The tribal conflicts after the 2007 election occurred far from the coastal resorts and main safari areas.

Kids, goats and gullies

Ecologically, Kenya is very stressed. Though population growth has recently fallen, it is still over 2.5 per cent per annum, with the median age about 18 years and over 42 per cent of the population under the age of 14. Polygamous families, where a man has more than one wife, are still common, and in spite of the ravages of AIDS the population continues to grow.

Although the towns and cities expand alarmingly, it is still the aspiration of every Kenyan to have his own *shamba*, a small piece of land where crops are grown and where he or she will eventually return to the

Degraded land near Magadi

earth at burial. However, the amount of useable land is finite, with highly marginal areas already in use. The land is often reduced to semi-desert, especially where goats and sheep graze. Where boreholes are drilled, a lowering of the water table depletes vegetation even further.

In times of limited water resources, available water holes become a magnet for herds, but the areas around them are quickly destroyed by overgrazing. Everywhere the forests are also under attack, for firewood, charcoal production and for building materials. Remove the trees, and soil on the slopes is easily eroded. Everywhere the land is being destroyed.

Tourism has brought new problems, from over-development in the parks to clumsy flippers killing off the fragile coral reefs. Nevertheless, without tourism Kenya would have no national parks and most of its wildlife would have vanished. Population pressure along the edges of national parks and reserves requires that all these prohibited areas produce real financial spin-offs for local people in order to guarantee their long-term sustainability.

The story is by no means all gloom and doom. For example, in the

A new tree nursery supported by the African Conservation Trust

western end of the Masai Mara, the so-called Mara Triangle, a new management system is revolutionising the way in which wildlife areas are run. The infrastructure has been totally refurbished; the roads are regraded, anti-poaching measures are working, and, as important, payment to the local Maasai from gate receipts have increased manyfold, supporting schools, clinics and even Maasai university students.

Since 2003, the African Conservation Trust has been a leader in a campaign to reverse the awful deforestation which has occurred in Kenya since independence. Their vision is to get Kenya back towards the 15 per cent forest cover of 1960, in comparison with less than 2 per cent today, with tree-planting schemes and sustainable charcoal production.

www.projectafrica.com

Impressions

Kenya is one of those extraordinary crossroads countries that really does provide something for everyone and it can be difficult to work out an itinerary, or select a package, because there is just too much choice. This is a basic, subjective list of where to find the very best the country has to offer.

Planning your Itinerary

Some of Kenya's best beaches are in Watamu, just south of Malindi, with silver-white sand, rich coral reefs and little seaweed compared to the southern resort areas. If you are spending time on this part of the coast, the Malindi and Watamu areas are excellent for deep-sea fishing and spotting coastal birds, while Mombasa, Nyali and Lamu have the best food this side of Nairobi. Nyali is also known for its upbeat nightlife. For those interested in historical sights, Lamu, Gedi and Mombasa Old Town have a rich Arabic history with some good museums and old relics.

Less than a two hour drive from the coast is Tsavo West National Park, which is wonderful for birdwatching, boasting over 400 species. Further west is Amboseli National Park, with views of Mount Kilimanjaro, and great for birdwatching and game-viewing as it has a large concentration of wildlife in a relatively small area. North from

Amboseli, in the centre of Kenya, are the Aberdares, Mount Kenya and Mount Elgon – superb areas for heavy-duty mountain trekking, scenery and river fishing. Head even further north to Maralel and the Ewaso Nyiro River area for hiking, camel-supported walking safaris and to visit the traditional villages of the Samburu. Beyond Maralel in northern Kenya is Lake Turkana, with bleak, dramatic desertscapes and home to the fascinating Turkana and El Molo people.

South towards Nairobi you will find great food, nightlife and rich colonial history. The Rift Valley northwest of Nairobi is spectacular for birdwatching, particularly Lake Baringo, with over 300 species including flamingoes and pelicans. The nearby Limuru area has scenic views over the Rift Valley escarpment and volcanoes. The Masai Mara National Reserve in the southwest is the best bet for game-viewing all year round, and particularly during the wildebeest migration (July–October);

Fishing boats pulled up on to the sandy beach near Malindi

while you are there, visit the villages of the nomadic Maasai who live in and around the reserve.

From the Rift Valley, heading further west into the Kenyan Highlands towards Lake Victoria, is Kisii, with views of intensively farmed terraces of tea plantations, the Kakamega Forest with its rare, rainforest bird species, and fantastic fishing in Lake Victoria.

Living with Kenya
Etiquette

On the whole, Kenyans are extremely polite, friendly and hospitable people. Always ask after the person's health and introduce yourself at the start of any proper conversation. Call a man *Bwana* (Mister) or a woman *Mama* (Mother or Madam), as a term of respect.

In the higher levels of society – and in white homes – Western rules of hospitality apply; if you are invited for a meal, take a small gift. But if you are invited into a village home, be prepared to eat and live as the family does and don't reject their food once you have accepted the invitation. Offer to pay for your board and, above all, remember that these are poor people. Don't abuse their welcome by living at their expense for days on end.

Africans touch more than Westerners do. They always shake hands on meeting and men will often hold hands in the street. This is not a sign of anything romantic, but simply of trust. You may be asked some staggeringly personal questions, but this is usually only curiosity, so deflect them with a smile and don't get upset. Race is the one truly touchy area and most Africans prefer to avoid the subject altogether. Their memory stretches back to colonial days and they can be quick to find offence even where none is intended.

The lifestyle is casual, but do not wander around the towns in beachwear. The upmarket city hotels may ask men to wear a jacket and tie after sundown. The coastal region is almost solidly Muslim and nude or topless sunbathing is a grave insult as well as being illegal.

The hassle factor

One of the most tiring aspects of the country is the general belief that all Westerners are super-rich. In some places, especially downtown Nairobi and in some tourist locations, beggars and people selling all kinds of wares are common. There are also many 'street children', often glue-sniffing. Your heart will bleed at the very real need surrounding you, but for the sake of your own sanity and solvency, you must have ironclad resolution and only give when you really want to.

If you do show any interest in buying, the price will be set according to what they think you might be prepared to pay and you will find yourself involved in protracted haggling, often with half a dozen people. Once you do eventually buy from one, the next will step forward to try and persuade you to buy from them as well. They refuse to accept that if you have already bought ten bracelets, you do not need any more, and will point out patiently that you have not yet bought a bracelet from them. There are no easy answers.

Language

Kenya has 40 tribes, all with their own languages. The official language of the country is Kiswahili (Swahili), which is spoken by almost everyone except a few

of the nomads. English is almost as widely spoken, however, and unless you are way off the beaten track, you will always find someone who speaks enough to help you. On the coast you will also find that resort receptionists and the souvenir sellers often have a smattering of German, French and Italian. Surviving is easy, but it is considered good manners to learn at least a few words of Swahili as a token gesture.

Servants

Kenyan society still survives, to some extent, in a colonial mode and unless you are roughing it in the cheapest possible way, get used to being surrounded by fleets of servants. Even mid-range camping trips regard as essential a driver, a cook and sometimes a couple of other people to collect firewood, put up tents and heat water. Most of them speak very good English and are a mine of useful and interesting information. If you are an independent traveller, always remember the value of having a ranger with you, both for spotting wildlife and for keeping you out of trouble.

It is easy to get used to wallowing in luxury, but do remember that the staff work long, very hard days. They will stay on duty until you go to bed, and they will rarely refuse to do anything you ask of them, even if they know that it is not sensible. They have to obey your wishes or risk losing their jobs. It is up to you to think of their comfort as well as your own.

A Maasai mother wearing traditional beadwork jewellery

Women travellers

Although it is not uncommon to see women travelling alone in Kenya, those who live permanently in the country would regard it as foolhardy. Hijacking and rape are relatively common. It is advisable for women not to go out alone at night and to restrict daytime activities on their own to busy areas.

Getting around

Look at a map of Kenya, and the country seems remarkably accessible, with highways, main roads and plentiful minor roads, a good rail network and numerous airfields. Nor are distances too long. All things are relative, however, and something marked as a highway in Kenya is probably the equivalent of a minor B road in Europe. It might even be marked as the main road simply because it is the only road. A 200km (124-mile) journey might take three hours, but it might also take three days.

By air

By far the easiest and fastest way to get around is by air, often in small planes that offer spectacular views. There are reasonably priced scheduled flights to most towns and game parks and even hiring a charter flight is not excessively dear if several of you share the cost. For small aircraft, Wilson Airport in Nairobi is deemed the busiest in Africa.

By rail

While the railway looks impressive, there are only three trains a week each way on both the Nairobi–Mombasa line and the Nairobi–Kisumu line. They are all evening departures leaving Nairobi on Monday, Wednesday and Friday, and

All *matatus* now have yellow stripes

returning on Tuesday, Thursday and Sunday. A rail journey is, however, an experience in itself (*see p144*).

By road

Though there have been improvements over the last few years, especially since 2002, Kenyan roads are often in a terrible state of disrepair. Kenyan politicians would do well to visit the superb new road from Arusha to Ngorongoro, the equivalent jewel to Masai Mara in Tanzania's tourist crown. The Rift Valley to Narok section of the main road to the Masai Mara, awful for a number of years, is now close to completion after reconstruction.

In general, public transport continues to be crowded, fast and dangerous. Corruption means that operators get away with poor standards of maintenance on buses and *matatus* (a kind of shared taxi service). Horrendous accidents are all too common.

The best way to get around safely and to see the country is to join an organised safari with a reputable company. The standards of both vehicles and of driving are normally very high.

For more information on getting around, *see pp178–9 & 186–7.*

Health and safety in Kenya
Health

In the pecking order of developing countries, Kenya is one of the safest and most hygienic, and as long as you are sensible you stand little chance of being ill. Nevertheless, this is a tropical country that is host to a wide range of diseases, many unpleasant and some fatal, and as a Westerner, you will have little or no natural immunity.

A full set of inoculations is essential and should include protection against yellow fever, typhoid, tetanus, hepatitis and polio. Start the course two months prior to your visit. Secondly, and crucially, take anti-malarial tablets, starting the course before you come to Kenya. Malaria is endemic and can be deadly. As the pills are not 100 per cent reliable, also arm yourself with a supply of repellent, mosquito coils and a mosquito net, and cover yourself up in the evenings. The best way to avoid getting malaria is not to get bitten.

Most Kenyans who can afford to now drink bottled water, which is easily available. Tap water in the major towns is supposedly safe. Once out of town, or lower down the social scale, don't ever drink tap water, unless you purify it yourself. At tourist establishments, food is usually scrupulously hygienic but, again, once outside the cocoon be sensible about what you eat. Don't swim in any natural fresh water because you risk picking up bilharzia, and don't walk around barefoot, as there are numerous small, nasty worms and insects on the ground. Abstain from casual sex unless you wish to put yourself at risk of contracting HIV/AIDS.

If you get any open wounds, treat them with antiseptic and cover them

Ballooning over the Mara River in the Masai Mara

up. If bitten by any animal, get treatment for rabies immediately. Take a pack of sterile needles and use them if you need an injection. If you need a transfusion, go to the best possible hospital, or preferably, return home first. If you are ill after you get home, remember to tell your doctor you have been in the tropics.

Safety and security

Most visitors will experience no problems at all, especially if they follow normal precautions: use hotel safes where provided; don't flaunt your wealth; carry as little money as possible; don't go walkabout at night. However, as with many resorts worldwide where the contrast between tourist wealth and the poverty of the local people is so huge, the traveller is occasionally targeted.

In town, you are most at risk from muggers and pickpockets. Wearing a money belt will not necessarily help as the more determined muggers simply slash through the strap. Whenever possible, leave valuables in the hotel safe, don't take more money than you need, and, if stopped, hand it over. NEVER resist. It is better to end up poorer than in hospital. Use a handbag with a zip and shoulder strap for slinging diagonally and carry your wallet in an inside or front pocket. Check with locals about which areas are safe and, most importantly, never walk anywhere after dark. Take a taxi even if you are only going a couple of blocks.

In the rural areas, Kenya's chief problem is bandits, most of whom are armed refugees from its neighbouring states Sudan, Ethiopia and Somalia, all of which have, or have had, severe problems of famine, drought, or civil war. Security within the national parks has been stepped right up and these are now safe, though remoter areas such as Meru and Kora may still sometimes be a problem. There are problems on some roads, however, and tourist buses are occasionally held up at gunpoint. Just bear in mind that the country is desperate to ensure that tourists are safe, and is doing everything in its power to mop up the bandits. A convoy system operates on some of the more dangerous roads while tourists are advised to avoid some areas altogether.

SNAKES

Although snakes are common in the wild, the average visitor will never see one. Even those who work permanently in the bush will see snakes only a few times a year. Most are only active at night, and spend their days sleeping in a shady place under rocks or in the bushes.

At night it is sensible to take precautions while you are walking around, on your way to and from dinner, for example. Always use a torch unless the paths are very well lit.

The most common snakes which may be a serious problem are puff adders, which are sluggish and, unlike most other snakes, do not tend to get out of the way. It is therefore sensible not to walk in the dark without a light.

So, the danger from snakes is very small, but real. Be sensible. Remember, if you do happen to see a snake, you can be sure it will be much more frightened of you than you are of it.

Listen carefully to what the locals say and take their advice. If you are travelling independently, hire a car with a driver and always make sure you reach your destination well before dusk.

Surviving in the wild

The number of tourists suffering injury from animals is tiny. Nevertheless, one needs to be reminded of a few basic 'truths'. National parks are not zoos, and the seemingly placid animals are truly wild and therefore dangerous. Within the grounds of your lodge or in your vehicle you are safe, but it is vitally important to follow simple guidelines. In the national parks and on safari, you will be shepherded around by guides and game guards and will often feel frustrated by seemingly pointless rules. Just remember that they are there for a purpose – to protect your life:

• Do not get out of the car near animals, no matter how dopey they seem. The serene-looking hippo grazing on the mudflats could literally chomp you in half if she feels her calf is under threat.

• Never feed any wild animal, no matter how cute or persistent. That sweet little monkey has razor-sharp teeth that can bite to the bone.

• If you are out of your vehicle and your guide tells you to move, move first and ask questions later. His eyes are far better at spotting well-camouflaged animals than yours and he could have seen a lion in that nearby clump of grass.

• If you go out walking, always wear trousers and sensible shoes, watch where you put your feet and hands, and check the ground or the rock before you sit down. You could find yourself confronted by a snake, scorpion or poisonous spider.

• If you do get bitten by anything, get immediate medical help. Some snake bites can kill within 30 minutes. Treatment for an animal bite should include a tetanus booster and rabies shots.

• If camping, shake out your sleeping bag before you get in, and tap out your shoes in the morning. Spiders and scorpions find these welcome retreats!

This section may sound alarmist. Please remember while reading it that Kenya is a fabulous country and that

A fish eagle, talons extended, swoops down on its unsuspecting prey

your journey will be one of the greatest experiences of your life. Don't let the need for a little common sense put you off going. For more detailed practical information, *see pp174–89*.

Photography

Kenya is a photographer's paradise. The scenery is amazing, the people are highly photogenic and the access to animal life is unsurpassed.

Most photographers have now 'gone digital', giving many advantages over film, and there are some common-sense tips to follow.

Make sure you bring enough batteries, or rechargeable facilities. Have enough memory cards or a suitable lightweight storage facility for your images. Ensure your lens system is good enough for animal or bird close-ups; 300mm minimum or equivalent is recommended.

If you are a film user, make sure you bring enough film; you are likely to need twice as much as you think. Keep your film cool, in the cool box if your safari vehicle has one. Overheated film can seriously damage picture quality.

Whichever system you use, ask your driver–guide to switch off the engine when you are photographing animals. Also, place the camera on a beanbag or similar when you are using a telephoto or zoom lens for those sought-after close-up shots.

Finally, take adequate lens-cleaning materials with you; in some locations it can get very dusty.

The Kenyan people have learned their photographic value all too well and almost nobody will let you take a picture of them without cash up front. This can even apply if you are shooting general street scenes or you happen to include people by accident in the background of a shot. The Maasai and Samburu are particularly hot on this, and people who have tried to take a couple of surreptitious pictures have ended up at the wrong end of a spear. If you want to photograph the people, ask them first as a matter of courtesy and be prepared to negotiate a price.

Taking photos of anything to do with the police, military, or the state is strictly illegal and you could lose your film, your camera, or even end up in jail.

Of the common animals, elephants are easiest to photograph

Nairobi

In May 1899, construction of the East African Railway (see pp142–3) reached a high plateau, known to the Maasai as Nyrobi (the place of cool waters). It had glutinous black soil and was swampy and fever-ridden, but it was the last flat land before the Rift Valley and a suitable site for a railhead. By July, its population was nearing 20,000.

In 1900, Nairobi officially became a town. In 1903 Thomas Cook became the official agent of the East Africa Railway Company. In 1907, the town became capital of British East Africa. By the 1950s, it had acquired a glamorous bohemian image that fed on the great Hollywood stars and titled aristocracy who flocked here on safari. Today, Nairobi has a population of just over 3 million. In the tiny tree-lined city centre, peeling colonial buildings huddle under sharply pristine skyscrapers. On the land which the former colonialists chose not to use for building – usually malarial river bottoms – enormous slums such as Kibera and Mathare have grown up, housing hundreds of thousands at incredible population densities.

Nairobi is all things to all people – the start of a dream; and the epitome of despair. You can buy anything here from Gucci watches to *foie gras*. Those that don't have money are mainly concerned with extracting it from those that do. Most visitors see it as a convenient stop between the airport and game parks.

City Park

Created in 1904 as Nairobi's first public park, this is a lush, cool 120ha (297-acre) area of mature forest reserve and wonderful gardens. It is home to the **Boscawen Memorial Orchid**

SECURITY

Sadly, the streets of downtown Nairobi are now among the least safe in the whole of Africa and we offer some simple advice:
- Never walk around anywhere in downtown Nairobi at night.
- Even during daylight hours, a walkabout in central Nairobi is out of the question. It is certainly worth visiting, but you should take a *licensed* taxi, even for the shortest journey.
- Do not flaunt your wealth. Cameras, watches, jewellery, mobile phone, money-belt, etc.
- If you are mugged, do not resist.

Having said all of this, the places you are likely to be on your visit, such as your hotel, lodge, on safari and at the airport, are normally pretty safe.

Nairobi, the garden city

art, with revolving displays by some 30 artists from across Africa as well as regular solo exhibitions of paintings and sculpture.
Standard St, Tel: (020) 221 5321. www. gallerywatatu.com. Open: Mon–Fri 10am–5pm. Free admission.

Kenyatta International Conference Centre
Built in 1974, this 28-storey (105m/ 344ft) building is Kenya's only major conference venue. It has an auditorium for 4,000 and is also the headquarters of KANU, for many years Kenya's ruling party. There are spectacular views across the city from the rooftop walkway.
City Square. Regular escorted tours run Mon–Fri 9.30am–6pm. Admission charge.

National Archives
The archives are housed in neoclassical splendour in one of Nairobi's oldest buildings (built in 1906 for the Bank of India). The entrance hall contains a fascinating jumble of art heaped like an Aladdin's cave. The private collection of former Vice-President Joseph Murumbi, it ranges from Persian carpets and Indian chests to masks and drums from across the continent, together with a number of paintings. Upstairs, an uninspired exhibition of archive material has some interesting information on Kenyan heroes and national emblems, but concentrates rather too heavily on politicians.

Collection and a war cemetery containing the graves of 97 East African soldiers, mainly from World War II. More cheerfully, it also has a children's playground in a sunken garden, a maze and a bandstand. Be careful in daylight and don't go in after dark.
City Park Rd, off Limuru Rd, 3.5km (2 miles) northeast of the city centre. Open: Mon 10am–6pm, Fri 7am–2pm, Tue–Thur & Sat–Sun noon–6pm. Admission charge.

Gallery Watatu
A commercial gallery, this is one of a handful of places to see good quality

Nairobi city centre

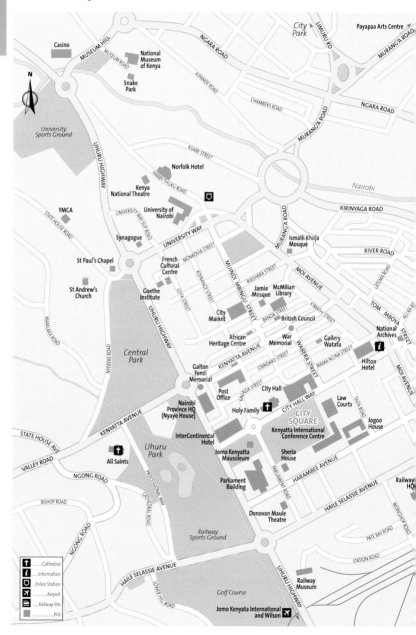

Moi Ave, opposite the Hilton Hotel.
Tel: (020) 222 8959. Open: Mon–Fri
8.15am–4.15pm, Sat 8.15am–1pm.
Admission charge.

National Museum of Kenya

An excellent, wide-ranging museum that
is the one essential sightseeing stop in
central Nairobi. It has the normal
selection of geological displays and dead
birds and animals. The most famous of
these is the life-size model of Kenyatta's
favourite elephant, Ahmed, from
Marsabit. Placed under 24-hour guard
by presidential decree, the elephant
became a national symbol of the fight
against poaching. He died of natural
causes in 1974, between the age of 55
and 62, with massive tusks a full 3m
(10ft) long and weighing 67 kilos
(148lb) each.

The highlight of the museum is the
Prehistory Hall. Here are the skulls
which have shaped the generally
accepted theory of prehistory, pushing
back the origins of man over 2.5 million
years. Also on display is the most
complete early skeleton ever found,
a *Homo erectus* boy, dating back about
1.6 million years. Along with the clear
explanations of East African prehistory,
with their mind-boggling dates, there
are copies of some of Tanzania's finest
rock paintings, made by Mary and
Louis Leakey in 1951; a section on
Richard Leakey's Koobi Fora
excavations (*see pp130–31*); and a series
of tableaux suggesting how our earliest
ancestors looked and lived.

Other interesting galleries, designed to interpret the heritage of Kenya and stimulate learning, include displays on the lifestyles and traditions of all Kenya's major tribes and a set of beautiful botanical paintings by Joy Adamson of *Born Free* fame (*see pp59 & 126–7*).

Museum Rd, off Museum Hill. Approx 2km (1¼ miles) northwest of the city centre, off Uhuru Highway. Tel: (020) 374 2161. www.museums.or.ke. Open: daily 9.30am–6pm. Guided bird tours every Wed at 8.45am. Admission charge.

Parliament Building

This rather disappointing 1930s building is the home of Kenya's single parliamentary house. The interior is more imposing, however. Among its artistic treasures are the 1968 statue of Kenyatta in the forecourt; the wooden panel on the landing, made by the local Kabete School in the 1950s, with each of its 32 pieces in a different local hardwood; and the series of 49 tapestries in the Long Gallery. Presented by the East African Women's League in 1968, the tapestries tell the colonial history of Kenya. Jomo Kenyatta (*see box, p25*) is buried in a mausoleum in the gardens, constantly attended by a guard of honour.

Parliament Rd. Tel: (020) 221 291. Phone the Sergeant-at-Arms for an appointment to tour the building or for a seat in the public gallery. Free admission.

Payapaa Arts Centre

Founded by one of Kenya's leading artists, the effervescent and enthusiastic Elimo Njau, this is a working artists' studio used by painters and sculptors. It also has a permanent collection and sales gallery. The aim of the centre is to promote a real creativity that will lift Kenyan art out of its current rut. A motto above the main door reads 'Copying puts God to sleep'.

Ridgeways Rd, off Kiambu Rd. About 8km (5 miles) northeast of the city centre. Tel: (020) 512 257. Open: daily 9am–5pm. Admission charge.

Railway Museum

This fascinating museum is dedicated to the history of the 'Lunatic Line' (*see pp142–3*). Numerous photographs and other memorabilia are used to chart the railway's past, such as the seat which was attached to the locomotive's cow-catcher to give distinguished visitors, including Winston Churchill and Theodore Roosevelt, the very best possible view. Outside are countless old engines and carriages, many in sad need of restoration. Look for number 12, the carriage in which the ill-fated Charles Ryall sat up one night, waiting for the man-eating lion which was terrorising the work gangs during the building of the line. The unfortunate man fell asleep and was dragged from the coach to become the lion's next meal.

Uhuru Highway. Tel: (020) 221 211. Open: daily 8.30am–4.30pm. Admission charge.

Vintage steam engine at the Railway Museum

Snake Park

A small park with a varied selection of East African snakes, from pythons to mambas; tortoises and crocodiles; and a small aquarium to introduce you to the freshwater tilapia which you will see more frequently on your dinner plate.

Beside the National Museum on Museum Rd, off Museum Hill, 2km (1¹/4 miles) northwest of the city centre, off Uhuru Highway. Tel: (020) 742 131/4. Open: daily 9.30am–6.30pm. Admission charge.

Uhuru Park and Central Park

Of no interest in horticultural terms, this large green area is one of Nairobi's favourite weekend hang-outs. The focal point of Uhuru Park is a small boating lake, while Central Park is dominated by the **Nyayo Monument**, built in 1988 to mark the first decade of President Moi's rule. Its vast octagonal plinth is topped by the peaks of Mount Kenya, from which bursts Moi's clenched fist holding a swagger stick. The hill behind the monument offers a tremendous view of the Nairobi skyline.

The two parks stand together beside the Uhuru Highway and separated by Kenyatta Ave. Open: all hours, but unsafe alone or after dark. Free admission.

NAIROBI ENVIRONS
Karen
Karen Blixen Museum

Karen Blixen (Isak Dinesen) lived in this low, stone house on her 2,428ha (6,000-acre) coffee farm from 1914 to 1931. Today, it is set in formal gardens while the farm itself has become the upmarket suburb of Karen, named after the author. Inside the house are a few of her own paintings and photographs, but most of the furniture was left behind by the producers of *Out of Africa*, the film version of her autobiography, along with the clothes worn by Meryl Streep (*See p53*).
Karen Rd. 18km (11 miles) southwest of Nairobi via the Ngong Rd. Tel: (020) 882 779. www.museums.or.ke. Open: daily 9.30am–6pm. Admission charge.

Ngong Hills

A popular area among colonial settlers, these beautiful, knuckle-shaped hills on the Nairobi skyline were made famous by Karen Blixen. Her lover, Denys Finch Hatton, who was killed in an air crash, is buried here. There are public footpaths along the top from where there are wonderful views (*see also pp52–3*). Check the security situation before setting out and don't go alone.
25km (15½ miles) southwest of Nairobi. The road is tarred as far as Ngong town. After that, 4WD is advisable in wet weather. Admission charges for the Finch Hatton Memorial and the summit.

Langata (*see map p53*)
The Bomas of Kenya

Slightly disappointing African folk centre. Numerous small tribal villages line the paths, but most are empty and those tribes present are far more interested in selling souvenirs than in explaining their lifestyle. The demonstrations of traditional African dance in the auditorium are more fun.
Forest Edge Rd, 10km (6 miles) southwest of Nairobi off the Langata Rd. Tel: (020) 891 801. Open: Mon–Fri 9am–5pm, Sat–Sun 1–6pm. Dance demonstrations 2.30pm Mon–Fri,

Karen Blixen's House, now a museum

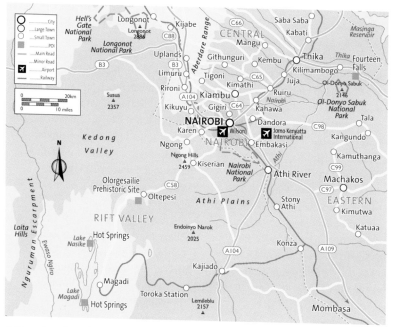

3.30pm Sat–Sun, & some evenings. Admission charge.

Butterfly Centre

Part of the African Butterfly Research Institute, this super education centre includes a 450sq m (4,844sq ft) greenhouse full of native butterflies and tropical plants, plus a gift shop and an outdoor restaurant.

Dagoretti Rd, 1km (⅔ mile) north of Karen. Tel: (0722) 363 288.

Langata Giraffe Centre

The highlight of this delightful conservation and education centre is the head-height platform which allows you eyeball to eyeball contact as you hand-feed a small herd of Rothschild giraffes. The centre was set up in 1975 to protect these rare animals. There are now around 500. There is a bird sanctuary and nature trail next door.

Gogo Falls Rd, Langata, 18km (11 miles) southwest of Nairobi. Access off Bogani Rd, via either Karen Rd or Langata Rd. Tel: (020) 891 658.

www.giraffecenter.org. Open: daily 9am–5.30pm. Admission charge.

Mamba Village

Attractions include crocodiles, an ostrich farm, camel rides, a restaurant, bar and gift shop.

Off Langata Rd. Tel: (020) 891 765.

Nairobi National Park

This was the first of Kenya's many national parks, declared as such in 1946, after having served time as a game reserve, Samburu grazing land and a military firing range. The park covers an area of 120sq km (46sq miles) between the city and the Athi River. Many of its larger mammals were reintroduced after World War II, but it now boasts some 80 species of mammal and 500 species of bird. Early morning and evening game-viewing is best. This is also the headquarters of Kenya Wildlife Services. *Langata Rd. 8km (5 miles) southeast of the city centre. Tel: (020) 602 345, (020) 501 181. www.kws.org. Entrances on Langata Rd (main gate and Langata gate) and the Airport Rd (east gate). Open: daily 6am–7pm. Admission charge.*

Nairobi Safari Walk

This educational showcase for Kenya's biodiversity opened in February 2001. Its 11ha (27 acres) cover three ecosystems – wetlands, savannah and forest. *Langata Rd. 8km (5 miles) southwest of Nairobi, at the main gate of the national park. Tel: (020) 602 345, (020) 501 181. www.kws.org. Open: daily 8.30am–5.30pm. Admission charge.*

Ostrich Park

This is populated by birds of all ages, from balls of fluff to tourist-hardened veterans. There are also excellent craft workshops here.

Near the Giraffe Centre, Langata Rd. Tel: (020) 891 051. Open: daily 9am–6pm. Admission charge.

Uhuru Gardens

A major iconic location for Kenyans, but not much to see for tourists. At this site, in 1963, Kenya gained its independence. The ornamental gardens have a statue of 'freedom fighters', together with a musical fountain. *Langata Rd, near Wilson Airport and Carnivore. Open: 24 hours. Free admission.*

Village Market, Gigiri

A favourite with Nairobi's UN and NGO crowd. There's a Masai Market on Fridays – waterslides, bowling, 18 restaurants and a cinema. *On the road to Limuru.*

Limuru (*see map p49*)

Set high on the rim of the Rift Valley, Limuru is one of those odd, charming, colonial hangovers that seem more English than England. Now it is most famous as the Kenyan headquarters of the ubiquitous Bata Shoes. All around are tightly terraced Kikuyu farms, and pine, coffee and tea plantations. In nearby **Tigoni** is the **Kentmere Club**, one of the least spoilt of the old colonial country clubs, **Kiambethu Tea Farm**, which can be toured by prior arrangement, and some charming 15m (49ft) high waterfalls, best seen from the grounds of the Waterfalls Inn.

The tumbling, muddy waters of the Athi River at the Chania Falls, Thika

mining centre for salt and soda ash. **Olorgesailie Prehistoric Site** Discovered by Dr Louis Leakey in 1942, this fine Stone Age site was almost continuously occupied from 200,000 to 150,000 BC. There are few visible remnants of the settlement, but a small site museum houses some of its many animal fossils and Stone Age tools.

The site is 80km (50 miles) and the lake 120km (75 miles) southwest of Nairobi. Open: 9.30am–6pm. Admission charge for both. Take a 4WD vehicle equipped with spare fuel and water.

On the way back to Nairobi, stop in at **Thogoto**, near Kikuyu town, to see the tiny **Church of the Torch**, built by Scottish missionaries in 1898.

Limuru is 30km (19 miles) northwest of Nairobi on the old Naivasha Rd. The Kentmere Club (tel: (020) 202 1369. www.kentmereclub.com) is just off the main road in Tigoni, clearly signposted. Kiambethu Farm (tel: (020) 882 779. www.kiambethufarm.co.ke) is 3km (2 miles) from the Club. Admission charge.

Southern Rift Valley
Lake Magadi

This southernmost of Kenya's Rift Valley soda lakes (*see p57*), 600m (1,969ft) above sea level, is set in a ferociously hot landscape. The lake covers 100sq km (39sq miles), but is less than 1m (3ft) deep. Popular with flamingoes and pelicans, it is a

Thika

Elspeth Huxley's flame trees are long gone and today Thika is a dull industrial town. On the outskirts, the 25m (82ft) high **Chania Falls** are best seen from the Blue Post Hotel, a fine example of early 1900s colonial architecture.

Some 20km (12 miles) east of the town are the **Fourteen Falls**, a 27m (89ft) high, horseshoe-shaped cascade on the Athi River. Just beyond them is the **Ol-Donyo Sabuk National Park** (*www.kws.org. Open: 6am–7pm. Admission charge*), covering 18sq km (7sq miles) around a 2,146m (7,041ft) high extinct volcano. There are fabulous views from the top. The park is a birdwatcher's paradise and is home to a huge variety of birds. Watch out for large herds of buffalo.

Thika is 30km (19 miles) northeast of Nairobi. There are security problems, so take local advice.

Tour: Out of Africa

Karen Blixen begins Out of Africa *with the following, 'I had a farm in Africa, at the foot of the Ngong Hills … the geographical position and the height of the land combined to create a landscape that had not its like in all the world.'*

Allow 1 day.

Leave Nairobi via Haile Selassie Avenue which leads onto Ngong Road, keeping left at Dagoretti Corner, past the Race Course, through Ngong Forest and straight on at the Karen roundabout. Eventually you reach a T-junction at Ngong, at which you turn left to Kiserian. At Kiserian turn right and take the Magadi road. You will soon reach a summit on the road at the eastern end of the hills where, below you, a new and different Africa unfolds.

1 The Ngong Hills

This is 'corner baridi', literally 'cold corner'. To your right are the knuckle-shaped Ngong Hills, which feature so strongly in Karen Blixen's *Out of Africa*. If you have half a day, you can easily climb the hills, but it would be advisable to arrange an armed ranger from the Kenya Wildlife Services post, west of Ngong town, to accompany you.

Below you to the south is the Rift Valley and the Masai steppe. The land becomes open savannah, with poor grassland scattered with acacia trees.

Listen for the sound of the clinking bells of the scattered Maasai herds.

It seems amazing that so close to bustling Nairobi there can be such a different Africa. It is a truly beautiful place and gives a little insight into what Karen Blixen described at the start of her book. Stay and savour the moment. *Return to Kiserian, but then keep straight on towards Nairobi until you reach Langata Road. Turn left and continue until you reach Karen Road, at which you turn left again, past the Karen Club and golf course, until you see the Karen Blixen Museum on your right.*

2 The Karen Blixen Museum

Karen Blixen, originally from Rungsted in Denmark, lived here from 1914 to 1931. The house and grounds were used as the set for the film *Out of Africa* with Meryl Streep and Robert Redford.

The fittings in the house are largely from the film, but the museum gives a good idea of how it was 70 or 80 years ago in the suburbs of Nairobi, though

her coffee farm has long-since gone.
A short distance along Karen Road is the Karen Blixen Coffee House, a delightful pub, coffee house and restaurant, based around an old colonial house, where you can get refreshments or lunch (www.blixencoffeegarden.co.ke). Afterwards head right and then left into Bogani Road until you see the signs to the right for the Giraffe Centre.

3 Langata Giraffe Centre

Set up as a rescue and educational centre for the rare and endangered Rothschild's giraffe, this is a lovely place, where you can get within touching distance, at giraffe-head-height, of these beautiful animals (*see also p49*).
Tel: (020) 891 658.
www.giraffecentre.org. Head back towards Magadi Road via Bogani Road, continue northeast on Magadi Road. The

entrance to Nairobi National Park is about 1km (²⁄₃ mile) after the Langata–Magadi road junction.

4 Nairobi National Park

A visit to Nairobi National Park for a few hours up to 7pm is a lovely way to end your day, and there are some nice picnic places for practising the Kenyan tradition of the 'sundowner'.

The national park forms part of the boundary of Nairobi city and contains all the 'Big Five' animals except elephants. Indeed it is one of the remaining strongholds for black rhinos, and early evening is the best time to see them (*see also p50*).
Smart cards and top-ups for entry are available at the gate. Nowhere in the park is more than about 20 minutes from the gate, but you must be out by 7pm. Turn right onto Magadi Road for the city.

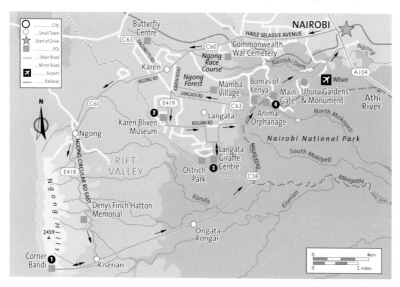

The Rift Valley

About 500 million years ago, there rose across Africa a vast mountain range that stretched from the Zambezi Valley to the River Jordan. About 20 million years ago, the central ground tore itself apart, creating a jagged rift across the continent. The land on either side erupted in a series of volcanic explosions making great mountains, while the valley floor gradually sank into a low flat plain, punctuated by volcanoes. This is the Great Rift Valley, one of the most incredible geological phenomena on the planet.

The Valley today

Punctuated by a long line of lakes, the present-day Rift Valley varies from uninhabitable desert to rich farmland. The majority of its volcanoes have been extinct for at least two million years,

Rift Valley and Central Highlands

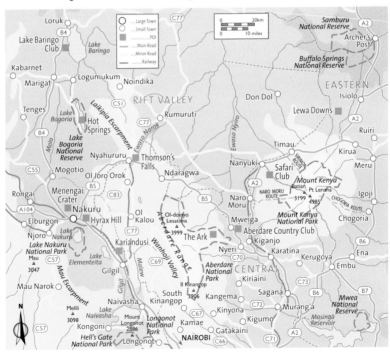

The view over the Rift Valley floor from the Nyambeni Hills

although many still have clearly defined craters on the summit. Nevertheless, subterranean rumbling continues and there are known to be some 30 active or semi-active volcanoes and many hot springs along its length. Only one hour from Nairobi is the volcano Longonot, which is believed to be dormant.

The Rift Valley is at its narrowest just north of Nairobi, a fact clearly visible in the stretch between the Mau Escarpment and the Aberdares. It is about 45km (28 miles) wide here, while the floor ranges from some 500m to 1,600m (1,640 to 5,250ft) above sea level. Its walls, sometimes barely visible, climb elsewhere to over 4,000m (13,100ft) high, with great slabs of broken rock sliding into the valley floor.

The area contains lakes, volcanoes and small game parks, and is heavily cultivated by both large-scale European farms and Kalenjin subsistence farms. During his presidency Moi built an excellent tarred road from Nairobi to his constituency near Baringo.

Kariandusi

Discovered by Louis Leakey in 1928, the Kariandusi Stone Age site was occupied around 10,000 years ago. There are guided tours of the excavations and a small museum (*www.museums.or.ke. Open: daily 9.30am–6pm. Admission charge*). The area is dominated by the massive diatomite mine next door. Diatomite is a chalky white material composed of microscopic marine

Fishing canoe on the freshwater lake at Baringo

fossils, which is used in brewing, in water filters and as an insecticide. Opposite, the small **Church of Goodwill** was modelled on a mission church in Zanzibar in 1949 by Nell Cole as a memorial for her husband, Galbraith, one of the great farming pioneers.
Old Nyahururu Rd, just east of Lake Elementeita, 120km (76 miles) northwest of Nairobi.

Lake Baringo

Baringo, the most northerly in a chain of lakes, is a large and beautiful expanse

RIFT VALLEY VIEWS

The Rift Valley is so staggeringly vast that it can be difficult to appreciate its size. The small planes that fly across the valley to the Masai Mara give a superb view, but it is clearly visible even from the high-flying international planes. By road, there are excellent viewing points just north of Limuru on the main Naivasha road and from the top of the Mau Escarpment on the Kericho road.

of fresh water, tucked under the high, eastern walls of the valley. A popular tourist stop, it is a superb centre for birdwatching, with over 450 species recorded. It is worth getting up at daybreak to join the dawn chorus. You will see almost everything, including the great African fish eagle and, since the recent fluctuations in Lake Nakuru's water levels, the great pink clouds of flamingos. Hippos roam the gardens at night, crocodiles bask in the shallows and monitor lizards sun themselves on the rocky shores.

The **Lake Baringo Club** offers boat trips, birdwatching walks guided by an ornithologist, camel rides and some watersports, although with crocodiles around, this may not be such a good idea. The club also runs the upmarket Island Camp on a small volcanic island and can arrange trips to the local Njemps tribal village and a nearby snake park.

The lake and club are just off the main Rift Valley Rd, 118km (73 miles) north of Nakuru. Reservations for the club via Let's Go Travel Ltd (see pp140–41).

Lake Bogoria

This long, skinny soda lake lies at the foot of the looming, black, 600m (1,969ft) high cliffs of the Laikipia Escarpment.

Bogoria does have flamingos and pelicans and the 107sq km (41sq mile) national reserve also houses one of Kenya's few herds of greater kudu. Yet the sheer peace and overwhelming physical beauty of the setting outweigh even these considerations. Towards the southern end of the lake are a series of dramatic hot springs with bubbling geysers, steaming streams and boiling pools, surrounded by richly patterned lichen-covered rocks. Be careful of stepping into hot water when walking around!

SODA LAKES

Soda lakes are formed in areas of inland drainage that have no outlet to either the sea or a larger lake. Trapped water evaporates in the intense heat and a crust of chemicals is left behind, mainly of highly alkaline sodium bicarbonate. There are still some hardy fish, but the only life that really flourishes here is microscopic algae and minute crustaceans. These, in turn, are the favourite food of numerous birds, and the soda lakes are superbly suited to the massive flocks of flamingos that crowd their shores.

Turn off the main road at Marigat, 20km (12½ miles) south of Lake Baringo and follow the signs for 30km (19 miles) through Logumukum to the park gate. Open: daily 6am–6pm. Admission charge.

Lake Elementeita

As recently as 12,000 years ago, this was part of a huge freshwater lake that also included Lake Nakuru. More recently, it was part of Soysambu, the vast ranch

The Rift Valley

Hot springs at Lake Bogoria

owned by Lord Delamere, one of the most influential of the early settlers. Today, Elementeita is a soda lake, which has some flamingos, but is largely ignored in favour of its larger neighbour, Lake Nakuru.

37km (23 miles) south of Nakuru. Open: 24 hours. Free admission.

Lake Naivasha and environs

Naivasha is the largest freshwater lake along the Kenyan section of the Great Rift Valley, constantly changing its size, but currently covering about 110sq km (42sq miles). Its name is a corruption of the local word *En-aiposha*, which means 'the lake'!

This was among the first areas to be settled by the colonists. Nearby **Wanhoji Valley**, on the western slopes of the Aberdares, is the original **Happy Valley**, a notorious spot given its nickname because of the large number of high-society, fast-living colonials who lived life to excess here in the 1930s. Down on the lake shore stands a house called Oserian (or the Djinn Palace) which became the centre of their revelries. It is still privately owned, and is not open to the public. From 1937 to 1950, Naivasha served as Nairobi airport, with Imperial Airways and BOAC flying boats taking four days for the journey from England. Today, much of the area is still intensively farmed and is particularly famous for cut flowers, strawberries and Kenya's only home-grown, drinkable wines. The lake is also a popular holiday playground for Nairobi and a superb centre for birdwatching, with over 400 species catalogued.

The turn-off for South Lake Rd is just before Naivasha town, 84km (52 miles) northwest of Nairobi. The road continues right around the lake, but the north and west sections sometimes need a 4WD vehicle.

Naivasha for a day trip

Naivasha is only an hour from Nairobi and is a favourite day trip or weekend destination for Nairobi residents. These are some of the things they do there:

- **Crater Lake Game Sanctuary**, for walking and camping.
- **Cresent Island**, for walking safaris and sailing.
- **Elsamere**, for lunch and accommodation.
- **Fisherman's Camp**, for food, camping, chalets, boat and bike hire.
- **Golf**, at the Rift Valley Course on the north side of the lake.
- **Hell's Gate National Park**, for walking safaris.

Crater Lake Game Sanctuary

Originally this was the estate of eccentric pioneer farmer Gilbert Colville and later of the notorious Lady Diana Delamere.

Though game viewing is limited, the crater lake is pretty and one can walk beside the lake or take an ox-wagon safari.

Follow South Lake Rd round to the western shore of Lake Naivasha. The entrance is about 7km (4 miles) beyond the end of the tarmac at Kongoni village. Open: daily 6am–6pm. Admission charge.

Elsamere

Joy and George Adamson bought this house in 1967 and lived here while struggling to return their pet lioness, Elsa, to the wild. It was here that Joy wrote her world-famous account of their efforts, *Born Free*. After her murder in Shaba National Park in 1980, the house was turned into a small museum and conservation centre. Elsamere offers accommodation and serves lovely meals.
South Lake Rd, Naivasha, opposite the Olkaria Geothermal Power Station. Tel: (050) 202 1055. www.elsatrust.org. Open: daily 3–6pm. Admission charge (includes a film show and hefty afternoon tea).

Hell's Gate National Park

The dramatic **Njorowa Gorge**, the ancient outlet from Lake Naivasha, has long since dried up, leaving a stark passageway between sheer, red, crumbling cliffs. Since the 1980s, it has been enclosed as part of a 68sq km (26sq mile) national park, one of a handful which allow you to walk unguided.

At the entrance to the gorge stands a craggy 25m (82ft) tall needle of rock called **Fischer's Tower**, after Gustav Fischer, who explored the area for the Hamburg Geographical Society in 1883. The loop between the two main gates is

22km (14 miles) long, but there is a shorter, 6km (4-mile) there-and-back nature trail from the Interpretation Centre. The western end of the gorge comes out into the **Olkaria Geothermal Power Station.** Attempts have been made to reintroduce the lammergeier, a species of vulture once commonly seen here, to Hell's Gate.
South Lake Rd, Naivasha. Tel: (050) 20510. www.kws.org. Open: daily 6am–6pm. Admission charge.

Lake Nakuru National Park

Set beneath the high cliffs of the eastern Rift, Nakuru is a soda lake (*see p57*) which constantly changes size and depth, depending on the seasonal rains. In the worst droughts (such as in early 1996), it may dry completely into a shimmer-white salt pan. An area of 188sq km (73sq miles) around the lake is fenced in as a national park and sanctuary for Rothschild giraffes and black rhinos. Lake Nakuru is also the

Lake Nakuru, almost solid with thousands and thousands of flamingos

best place in Kenya to view white rhinos, and in October 2009 the park was the first in Africa to be declared an Important Bird Area (IBA). It has a truly fantastic array of some 450 different species recorded, including endangered birds such as the Madagascar pond heron, the grey-crested helmet-shrike and the martial eagle.

When conditions are right, with sufficient water to support life without diluting salinity, the lake is home to one of Kenya's greatest visual experiences – the shimmering coral glow of up to 2 million flamingos dredging their way across the shallows. At other times, the birds gather at Bogoria or Elementeita.

Once down on the mudflats, you are hit by the full impact of this noisy, squabbling and smelly colony of greater and lesser flamingos and pelicans. Occasionally, if alarmed, they all take to the air in a cloud of beating salmon wings. It is a sight never to be forgotten. Remember to drive up to Baboon Rocks for the spectacular viewpoint.

The park entrance is 6km (4 miles) from Nakuru town, 158km (98 miles) northwest of Nairobi. Tel: (051) 224 44069. Open: daily 6am–7pm. Admission charge.

Hyrax Hill

Discovered by the Leakeys in 1926, this is a major Neolithic and Iron Age site, occupied from about 1000 BC to AD 300. The small museum includes finds from various nearby excavations. The main site is a walled hill fort on a spur with fine views across Lake Nakuru. There are few obvious physical remains and those with a serious interest should buy the excellent small guidebook.
Turn off the main road, about 3km (2 miles) southeast of Nakuru town. www.museums.or.ke. Open: daily 9.30am–6pm. Admission charge.

Menengai Crater

The second-largest intact volcanic crater in the world, Menengai's highest point is 2,242m (7,356ft) above sea level. The crater is several kilometres in diameter and plunges 483m (1,585ft) down from the rim. The mountain is surrounded by a 60sq km (23sq mile) nature reserve. It is possible to drive or walk the 8km (5 miles) from the main road to the summit and the view from the top is superb. Security is uncertain, so check on the situation before setting out.
The Menengai approach road turns off the Nyahururu Rd, just north of Nakuru town.

Mount Longonot

At 2,886m (9,469ft), this is the highest of the great Rift volcanoes. Part of a 52sq km (20sq mile) national park, its almost perfect circular crater, about 1km (^{2}/$_3$ mile) in diameter, is clearly visible from the main Rift viewpoint. The crater floor is flat, with its own rich ecosystem and steam gushing from crevices. Funnels of lava on the slopes have given the mountain its local name, Oloonong'ot ('the mountain of steep ridges'). Allow up to six hours for the

The cone of Mount Longonot, one of the Rift Valley's largest and youngest volcanoes

steep climb up from the ranger station and round the circumference of the rim. *60km (37 miles) northwest of Nairobi. Access is via the old Naivasha Rd, which turns off the new road just north of Limuru. Open: daily 6am–6pm. Admission charge.*

Nyahururu

The small, sleepy market town of Nyahururu ('the place where the waters run deep') is one of the highest settlements in Kenya (2,360m/7,743ft), and was founded with the arrival of the railway in 1929. The main reason to stop is the 72m (236ft) high **Thomson's Falls**, on the Ewaso Narok River.

In 1883, the British explorer Joseph Thomson named these falls after his father during his epic trek across the Central Highlands and the Rift Valley to Mount Elgon. He then looped back past Lake Victoria and across the southern plains.

The falls, which thunder into a rainbow-sprayed gorge beside the Thomson Falls Lodge, are sadly surrounded by hordes of souvenir sellers. There is a crumbling and slippery path to the bottom. If you do walk down, take great care. *50km (31 miles) northeast of Nakuru on the northern end of the Aberdares. Open: 24 hours. Admission free.*

The white tribe

There is an image of the Kenyan settlers as hard-living high-society misfits who spent their days stalking defenceless elephants and their nights bed-hopping. Among the early settlers, there was a surprising number of old school ties, and by the 1930s, the lifestyle of the upper-crust Happy Valley Set had become notorious. The majority of the country's white population was a very different breed, however. Hard-working farmers and administrators, many arrived after World Wars I and II as part of a government soldier-settler scheme, which gave cheap land to its war heroes. The early life was anything but comfortable as they forced the land into production almost by sheer willpower, living in shacks, dying of fever and often going bankrupt.

In the run-up to independence, the white population dwindled rapidly. While accurate statistics are not available, the numbers continue to fall. Of those that have stayed on, many are still on the land, while others are in the tourist industry. They have a comfortable life, on the whole, still retaining some of the trappings of the colonial era, such as large houses and servants. Europeans congregate together in suburbs such as Karen and Lavington. They often send their children to school abroad and they belong to clubs such as Karen and Muthaiga Country Club. Aware of their privileged position, they keep their heads down.

The other, larger grouping of white people is quite different, a floating population of expatriates and aid workers known as 'two-year wonders'. Some throw themselves into the 'African experience' with a vengeance; others live a ghetto-like existence, trying to pretend they have never left home. The Africans welcome the money they bring, but are bemused by them all. Numbers of aid workers are falling, as successive administrators seem unable to resolve

English-curriculum schools, such as Brookhouse, are still common

Colonial house built near Nyeri

the endemic problems of corruption and poor governance.

The Happy Valley refers to the area around Lake Naivasha and the Central Highlands – formerly the White Highlands – on which the British settlers chose to build their farms on account of it being fertile and well-watered. Much of the land is still owned by white Kenyans today but is the subject of a possible reclamation by the Kenyan government, to be returned to the original landowners, the Kikuyu.

The colonial town of Nyeri, to the east of the Aberdares mountain range, was the Happy Valley epicentre. Remnants of the colonial past are evident here, with the Aberdare Country Club, the Outspan Hotel and, in Thika, the Blue Posts Hotel – all of colonial heritage. Hugh Cholmondeley, Lord Delamere, was perhaps the most famous member of the Happy Valley settlers, and one of the first and most influential British pioneers in Kenya.

The Central Highlands

'Looking back on a sojourn in the African highlands, you are struck by your feeling of having lived for a time up in the air. . . Up in this high air you breathed easily, drawing in a vital assurance and lightness of heart. In the highlands, you woke up in the morning and thought: Here I am, where I ought to be.'

KAREN BLIXEN, Out of Africa, *1937*

Most people who have ever lived in the Central Highlands (*see map p54*) think them perfect. The Kikuyu regard the area as sacred land, given to them by God. The settlers looked at the rich earth, the tumbling mountain streams, felt the cool rush of the wind, and found a farmers' paradise. Most of the habitable land is between 1,800m and 3,000m (5,900 and 9,840ft) above sea level and almost everything can grow here, from tea and coffee, pine and eucalyptus on the higher slopes, to maize and oranges, pineapples and bananas on the lower. The Highlands are said to have one of the most perfect climates in the world, with just enough rain, warm days and crisp, cool nights. They are even free of many tropical diseases that blight the lower lands.

These days, few of the huge colonial estates remain, but those that do are quite spectacularly large, such as the massive **Del Monte pineapple plantation**, said to grow nearly a third of the world's pineapples. Most of the estates' lands have been returned to the Kikuyu people and carved up into intensively cultivated subsistence plots. Wherever you look, the scenery is a rich tapestry of steep terraces that carpet the hillsides in glowing green. Yet, however beautiful these are, the Highlands' crowning glories are its great mountains, the wild Aberdares and the cloud-covered, snow-capped summit of Mount Kenya.

THE ABERDARES

Formed by volcanic lava welling up through great fissures in the earth, the Aberdares are dramatically beautiful mountains, whose peak, Ol-Donyo Lesatima (3,999m/13,120ft), is the third highest in Kenya. The range runs roughly north to south, for about 60km (37 miles). Known to the Kikuyu as Nyandarua ('Drying Hide'), because of their resemblance to a skin over a drying frame, they were renamed in 1884 by Joseph Thomson, the first European to see them, after Lord Aberdare, president of the Royal Geographical Society. In 1950, a 767sq km (296sq mile) national park was created.

Several bands of distinctive vegetation wrap the mountains, from dense rainforest, through dense bamboo forest, to the weird alpine plants of the high moorlands. The lower slopes support a wide variety of animal life, from elephant, rhino and buffalo, to some rare species, such as the enchanting, chestnut-coated bongo antelope. However, the animals are too timid and the vegetation too thick for good game-viewing. (*See the map on p76*, Aberdare Mountain drive.)

Aberdare Country Club

An attractive corner of little England, this doubles as the local country club and a popular tourist hotel. Built on a precipitous slope, it has lovely gardens and superb views. The grounds also include a small game sanctuary and a golf course. Activities include walking, tennis, swimming, riding and fishing. *Mweiga, 10km (6 miles) north of Nyeri. Tel: (020) 600 800. Email: aberdare@wanachi.com. www.kws.org. Daily membership available for non-residents.*

The Ark

Built in the shape of an ark, this hotel is designed for close-up sedentary game-viewing, with raised platforms, a photographic bunker and floodlights powerful enough for night pictures. Situated in the Salient area on the western slopes of the Aberdares, it stands beside a large, swampy waterhole and artificial salt lick, surrounded by dense forest and cavernous valleys.

A little slice of home, England recreated at the Aberdare Country Club

Buffalo are frequent visitors to the Treetops waterhole

No access for private vehicles. Guests are picked up daily at 2.30pm from the Aberdare Country Club. Tel: (020) 216 940. www.fairmont.com/ark. No children under 7.

Italian Memorial Church

Looking as if it has strayed off a Tuscan hillside, this church was built in 1952 by the Italian government as a memorial to the Italian soldiers and prisoners of war who died in Kenya during both world wars (*see map p76*). There were several large POW camps in the country, including one at nearby Nyeri. It is a moving sight, the walls lined by hundreds of memorial plaques, many adorned with photos and mementoes left by relatives.

5km (3 miles) northwest of Nyeri. Open: daily 8am–5pm. Ask the caretaker to unlock the church. Free admission.

Outspan Hotel

A charming old colonial hotel with fine views across to Mount Kenya. The grounds contain a fascinating small museum dedicated to Lord Baden-Powell (1857–1941), founder of the Boy Scout movement, who lived here, in the cottage, Paxtu, from 1938 to 1941. He is buried in the graveyard of St Peter's Church, Nyeri.

Baden Powell Rd, Nyeri. Tel: (061) 203 2424. Ask at reception for admission to the museum. Admission charge. St Peter's Church, Nyahuru Rd (opposite the CalTec Garage on the road to Aberdan National Park HQ). Access to the grave is free.

Treetops

The original and most famous of the 'treetop' hotels, first inspired by Peter Pan and opened literally as a two-room tree-house in 1932. It was here, in 1952, that Princess Elizabeth heard of her father's death and her own accession to the British throne. It is now a much larger hotel, but is still on stilts overlooking a salt lick and waterhole for comfortable, night-time game viewing.

Tel: (061) 203 4914. www.aberdaresafarihotels.com. No access for private transport. Reservations via Aberdare Safari Hotels. Tel: (020) 445 2095; lunchtime pick-up from the Outspan Hotel.

MOUNT KENYA AND ENVIRONS

One of the largest single mountains in the world and the second highest in Africa, this snow-capped colossus bestrides the equator with a base 120km (75 miles) in diameter and its highest peak (Batian) soaring to 5,199m (17,057ft). The mountain, named Kere-Nyaga (literally either 'Mountain of Whiteness' or 'Mountain like Ostrich Feathers'), is said by the Kikuyu to be the home of the gods. The first European to see it was a German missionary, Johann Krapf, in 1849, but his discovery was howled down in disbelief. It was not until Joseph Thomson found the mountain again in 1883 that Krapf was finally vindicated. The great mountain has since given its name to the entire country. Mount Kenya National Park is now a World Heritage Site.

Mount Kenya is a volcanic cone which last erupted about 2 million years ago. Its crater has long since eroded away to leave smoothly curving slopes, while the craggy peaks at the summit are the last remnants of the hard volcanic core. The deep valleys around the summit have been carved out by glaciers. The retreat of Mount Kenya's glaciers (numbering 18 in 1883, now only 7 remain) is some of the best evidence for global warming over the last century.

For information on climbing Mount Kenya, see pp72–5.

Isiolo

Isiolo (1,250m/4,101ft) is a hot, dusty town below the dramatic escarpment which plunges down over 2,000m (6,562ft) from the Central Highlands. It acts as a gateway to the remote deserts of the northeast, and its population has swelled rapidly with the arrival of thousands of Somali refugees. It has a lawless, frontier town atmosphere, its streets often roamed by gangs of wild-eyed youths, high on alcohol, or *miraa* (a locally grown narcotic plant). Be very careful of security. If you plan to drive further north, check in with the local police point.

82km (51 miles) northeast of Nanyuki on the A2 (the Great North Rd).

The summit of Mount Kenya is a rare sight, clear only for a few minutes each morning

African Nativity in Murang'a Cathedral, a memorial to Mau Mau victims

Lewa

A combination of cattle ranch, private game park and rhino sanctuary, the 25,000ha (62,000-acre) Lewa Downs offers rich game viewing (although no lions), comfortable accommodation, a laid-back atmosphere, bush walks, horse rides, day and night game drives and birdwatching and, for an additional cost, sightseeing flights over Mount Kenya. Alternative accommodation is available at the nearby luxury Lerai Tented Camp.

Lewa Wildlife Conservancy, Isiolo. The entrance to the farm is about 20km (12½ miles) past the Meru fork on the Isiolo Rd. www.lewa.org. Booking via Bush and Beyond Ltd. Tel: (020) 600 457. www.bush-and-beyond.com

Meru

Founded originally as a centre for hardwood timber (the Meru Oak), Meru is now famous for potatoes and *miraa*. Known in the Middle East as *q'at*, the twigs of the *miraa* bush are a narcotic, legal in Kenya, producing a high that can lead to severe sleep deprivation. (*See pp126–7 for* Meru National Park.)

Meru Museum

This tiny, faded museum in the old District Commissioner's Office has interesting displays about the Meru tribe, a reconstructed village, gardens growing local medicinal herbs and a horrific little snake park and zoo.

Northeast corner of the Mount Kenya Ring Rd. The museum is just past the

town hall. *www.museums.or.ke.*
Open: Mon–Fri 9.30am–6pm,
Sat 9.30am–2pm. Admission charge.

Murang'a

The **Cathedral Church of St James and All Martyrs**, Murang'a, was consecrated in 1955 as a memorial to the many Christians who refused to take the blood-curdling oath of loyalty demanded by the Mau Mau independence guerrillas and were killed as a result. Inside is a series of murals translating the story of the Nativity to an African setting painted by leading Kenyan artist Elimo Njau. He now runs the Payapaa Arts Centre (*see p46*).
87km (54 miles) north of Nairobi at the foot of the Mount Kenya Ring Rd. The cathedral is on a hill above the town centre. Ask the caretaker to unlock the building. Free admission.

Nanyuki

A charming market town with tree-lined streets, Nanyuki has many old-fashioned colonial shops, of which the Settler Store, built in 1938, is the most famous. There is a large and lively market and a Spinners' and Weavers' Co-operative, where you can watch the women working the local wool and buy a variety of rugs, shawls and jumpers.

South of the town, at the big equator sign, crowds of souvenir sellers try to demonstrate how water swirls down the plug in different directions in the northern and southern hemispheres.
60km (37 miles) north of Nyeri on the

Mount Kenya Ring Rd. The Weavers' Co-operative is in the grounds of the Presbyterian Church, Nyeri Rd. Open: Mon–Fri 9am–5pm, Sat 9am–12.30pm. Free admission.

Animal Orphanage

This delightful institution is run by the William Holden Foundation as a conservation and education centre. You can spend hours playing with baby bongos, kept here as part of a captive breeding programme, tickling giant tortoises and cuddling bushbabies.
PO Box 35, Nanyuki.
Tel: (020) 221 6940.
www.animalorphanagekenya.org.
Turn right near the Nanyuki equator sign. Accommodation expensive. Day membership available, plus separate admission charge for the Animal Orphanage.

Mount Kenya Safari Club

An extraordinary oasis of unashamed luxury, this is one of the finest hotels in the world. Although the original house was built in the 1930s, it was the American film star William Holden who turned it into this Hollywood dream, with a visitors' book that reads like *Who's Who*. There are 40ha (99 acres) of impeccably manicured gardens roamed by peacocks and sacred ibis, a golf course, a tennis court that crosses the equator, and a 405ha (1,000-acre) private game ranch.
Nanyuki. Tel: (020) 221 6940.
www.fairmont.com

The Kikuyu

According to legend, Mogai (God), who lives on Kere-Nyaga (Mount Kenya), gave the Central Highlands to Gikuyu, founder of the Kikuyu tribe. Gikuyu settled happily and over the years had nine daughters, but no sons. So he went to Mogai for help and Mogai created nine men to be

Terraced fields in the Kikuyu heartlands of the Central Highlands

their husbands. From them sprang the nine clans of the tribe. To this day, Kikuyu people build their houses facing sacred Mount Kenya.

The Kikuyu are a Bantu tribe who settled in the area in the 16th century. Four hundred years later, the early settlers fixed their sights on this lush region. Blind to the complex system of land ownership at the very heart of Kikuyu civilisation, they saw only vast tracts of 'virgin' bush and failed to realise that every centimetre had an owner and was used in some way. They saw simple homes with an oral tradition and assumed these were a primitive and stupid people. They saw smiles and failed to see the bitter resentment of the dispossessed. Winston Churchill described them as 'light-hearted, tractable, if brutish children'. Almost to a man, the settlers misunderstood the Kikuyu culture.

On their part, the Kikuyu soaked up the missionaries' education, many converting to Christianity, and adapted easily to Western ways. Then they began to try to retrieve their stolen lands, first by founding nationalist organisations which sent emissaries to London, then resorting to the terror of Mau Mau (*see* History, *p23*). At independence, they claimed the government of Kenya.

Today, the tribe numbers nearly 7 million, most of whom still live amid the tight patchwork of terraced fields on the Highland slopes. Many have also adapted with glee to big business and city living.

Though lacking the political dominance of the Kenyatta era, the Kikuyu are still Kenya's single most powerful economic and political force.

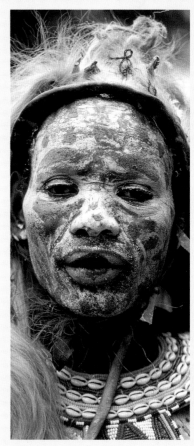

Kikuyu ceremonial dress is highly colourful and dramatic

Hiking up Mount Kenya

Mount Kenya has long, smooth slopes on three sides, and the climb to the ring of rocky peaks at the summit can be made by anyone of average fitness. The result of this accessibility is that numerous untrained and over-eager people, who have never before been at high altitude, behave without any regard for their surroundings and several of them die on the mountain every year. Act sensibly, however, and even if you come back dog-tired, wet and uncomfortable, it will be one of the greatest triumphs of your life.

The routes

There are eight accepted routes up the mountain, of which three are climbed regularly; Naro Moru to the west (the easiest and most popular, *see pp74–5*), Sirimon to the north and Chogoria to the east. The actual summit is Batian, at 5,199m (17,057ft), but to get there involves crossing the glaciers and high altitude rock climbing. The non-rock climbing treks all aim for Point Lenana, the third highest peak at 4,985m (16,355ft).

It is also possible to do either a circular walk around the peaks or to come back down a different route, but the latter should only be attempted by the very fit and experienced.

Staying healthy

There are two main health hazards on the mountain. The first is altitude sickness, which can strike anyone, no matter how young or fit, and in its acute form can kill. This is caused by climbing too fast, and the temptations

are enormous on these short and relatively easy routes. The climb can be accomplished in two to three days but, to be sure that you give yourself time to acclimatise, allow five. If you feel nauseated, over-exhausted, or have a severe headache, stop at once. If the symptoms get worse, head downhill immediately.

The second hazard is hypothermia, caused by getting too cold and run-

FURTHER INFORMATION

Mount Kenya Map
By Andrew Wielochowski and Mark Savage; 1:50,000 maps with excellent detailed notes on the routes.
Mount Kenya Mountain Guides and Porters Association
Tel: (062) 62015. www.gotomountkenya.com
Mount Kenya Mountain Lodge
(Serena) 42 double rooms.
Tel: (020) 711 077.
Mount Kenya National Park
PO Box 69, Naro Moru. *Tel: (0171) 2383.*
The Mountain Club of Kenya
PO Box 45741, Nairobi. *Tel: (020) 602 330; www.mck.or.ke*

down. Avoid it by keeping warm and try not to get wet or exhausted.

Supplies and porterage

For safety reasons, you are not allowed to climb solo. There are organised tours, but if you want a little independence, hire a full set of mountain equipment and a guide and/or porter at affordable rates.

You will need warm, windproof clothing, gloves, stout walking boots and plenty of socks, a good tent and sleeping bag, a stove and lots of high-energy food and drinks. Also take high UV-protection sunglasses, a hat and sunblock.

Mountain Rock Lodge

The lodge will organise everything for you.
15km (9 miles) south of Nanyuki.
Tel: (020) 224 2133.
www.mountainrockkenya.com

Naro Moru River Lodge

A comfortable hotel whose mountain shop hires out all equipment needed, and handles bookings for the mountain huts. Naro Moru town is the headquarters of the Mountain National Parks and the Guides and Porters Association.
PO Box 18, Naro Moru.
Tel: (020) 444 3357
www.alliancehotels.com

Hiking up Mount Kenya

Sunrise over Mount Kenya

Hike: Mount Kenya, the Naro Moru route

Mount Kenya is one of only a handful of great mountains whose summit is accessible to non-climbers. The Naro Moru route is the easiest ascent, but you still need to be fit and properly equipped. For more practical details, see pp72–3.

Allow up to 5 days.

Start at the Naro Moru River Lodge, 35km (22 miles) north of Nyeri on the Mount Kenya Ring Rd.

The lodge to the gate

This first 17km (10^1/$_2$-mile) stretch of the walk is relatively easy walking on roads; it is possible to hire a vehicle for the journey. The road leads through Naro Moru town, then turns right to start the climb through farmland. After 12km (7^1/$_2$ miles), you enter thick forest. As you near the gate, this turns into conifer forest and the last short section opens out again beside the park's airstrip.

The gate to the Met Station

The summit of Mount Kenya is a national park. You must pay your entry fees at the gate (2,400m/7,874ft). Be sure to spend time at the superb visitor centre just before the gate. If it has been raining, this is the last point accessible by vehicle; in good weather a 4WD vehicle can get as far as the Meteorological Station. About 1km

(^{2}/$_3$ mile) beyond the gate, you enter the thick tropical bamboo forest. After 7km (4 miles), the Percival Bridge crosses a deep ravine and 3km (2 miles) further on, you reach the Meteorological Station at 3,000m (9,843ft), the first overnight stop.

Met Station to Mackinder's Camp

This stage covers 12km (7^1/$_2$ miles), climbs 1,150m (3,773ft) and takes 6 to 7 hours. About 40 minutes after leaving the Met Station, the forest ends abruptly and you come out onto open moorland, with superb views (on good days) across the Aberdares and the Nyeri Valley. The next section, which takes about three hours, is known as the Vertical Bog – horribly soggy after rain, but not too bad in dry weather. Red and white markers show the path.

From now on, keep an eye open for the extraordinary moorland plants, such as giant groundsel, lobelias and heather. As you come out onto the ridge above the Teleki Valley, you should get your first clear view of the peaks. There are two routes across the valley; short(ish) and sharp on the left and longer and easier on the right. They join up on the far side for the last climb to Mackinder's Camp and the Teleki Hut, at 4,200m (13,780ft). Spend two nights here acclimatising.

To Point Lenana

The summit may peer out of the clouds for a few short minutes early every morning, so if you wish to make the summit in one bite and see the view, your day starts horribly early – around 3am! There is a climb of about 800m (2,625ft) (three to four hours) to the top. Take the main path past the ranger station and after 0.5km ($\frac{1}{3}$ mile), take the right-hand fork. This leads over another stretch of boggy ground around the head of the valley and up a large scree slope. At the top of the ridge, there are superb views of Lewis Glacier and the southeast face of Point Nelion. From here, the path crosses a rocky plateau before climbing up more scree to the Austrian hut at 4,790m (15,715ft). If taking five days, this is your last night's stop. From the hut, the last 200m (656ft) to the summit are straight up.

The journey down can be done in a single day.

Teleki Valley from Point Lenana, Mount Kenya

Drive: Aberdare Mountain

This route crosses the southern section of the Aberdares, reaching a height of 3,500m (11,483ft) and passing through some of Kenya's most spectacular scenery, with rich farmland, bamboo forest and alpine moorland. The road is the best in the National Park (tel: (0170) 55024), but even so, it should not be attempted except in a 4WD vehicle and is often closed completely after heavy rain.

Allow 1 day.

Start the drive from Nyeri town. Take the Nyahururu Rd north for approximately 5km (3 miles) and then turn left on to the road signposted to the Ruhuruini Gate and the Aberdare National Park. This leads past the Italian Memorial Church (see also p66) to reach Ihururu village. Turn right at the village, clearly signposted to Kimathi Secondary School. Fork right at each new turn after this. The gate is signposted, but the notices are not always easy to spot.

1 The approach road

The road is magnificent, climbing steadily through rich farmland, with wide vistas over countless small maize plots ringed by banana trees and huge open fields of velvet-smooth tea, broken by patches of eucalyptus and pine. *At the edge of the forest reserve, hoot for the gatekeeper to open the barrier.*

2 Ruhuruini Gate

Ruhuruini Gate, some 6km (4 miles) further on, is tucked into a secluded valley surrounded by vast stands of high bamboo. Once through the gate, the road winds ever more steeply around tight bends in the mountainside, with sharp falls and dramatic views over cavernous steep-sided valleys. It is impossible to see far into the dense undergrowth, but even the roadside displays a fantastic tapestry of gnarled trees dripping with Spanish moss, bamboo and wild flowers. Keep an eye open for animals, from buffalo to the timid bongo, or elegant troops of black-and-white colobus monkeys in the high branches. *As you reach the heights, above 3,000m (9,843ft), you come out on open moorlands. Shortly afterwards, the road forks. Turn left.*

3 The moorland

This is the only place in Kenya where the strange, giant alpine vegetation of the high moorlands is accessible by vehicle. It is a stark landscape, cool and often shrouded in mist. A turning to the left, just past the campsites, leads down to the access point for the 25m (82ft) high **Chania (Queen's Cave) Waterfall**.

Continue south for about 4km (2¹/₂ miles) to a crossroads, where you turn left. About 1km (²/₃ mile) on, the second turning on the left leads to the self-help fishing lodge, a simple cabin used as a base by keen trout fishermen. Keep on the main road for another 7km (4 miles).

4 Karuru and Gura Falls

A footpath to the left leads towards the 275m (902ft) high Karuru Falls and the 300m (984ft) high Gura Falls (the highest in Kenya), two thin, bright ribbons weaving down into the ravine near the confluence of the Gura and Karuru rivers. You should take a ranger with you if you plan to make the 6km (3³/₄-mile) walk there and back.

From here, the road turns west to cross the ridge, leading to Mutubio West Gate, still about 3,000m (9,843ft) high and the exit from the national park.

5 Rift Valley descent

The views get even more spectacular to the west, looking out over the forests to the Rift Valley, some 2,000m (6,562ft) below. The road hurls itself down the mountain in a series of switchbacks, plunging through the forests and out into farmland near **Wanhoji Valley** (the original 'Happy Valley'). Shortly after this, it joins the main road to Naivasha.

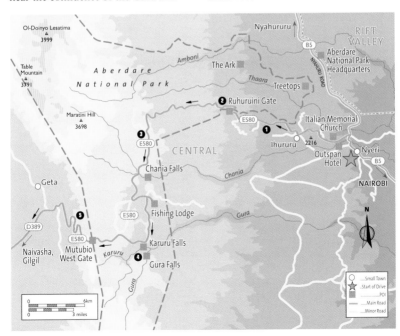

Western Kenya

West of the Rift Valley, stretching to the Ugandan border and Lake Victoria, is an area almost untouched by tourists. You will not find luxury lodges or organised safaris, but those prepared to make their own arrangements will find some of the most beautiful scenery the country has to offer.

The plains beyond the Mau Escarpment, which makes up the western wall of the Great Rift Valley, are made up of Kenya's oldest rocks, re-emerging from a lava plain that bears both gold and soapstone (*see p6*). In the south, around the Masai Mara, the climate is dry and the vegetation scrubby.

Further north, Lake Victoria has created its own microclimate. Warm and humid with year-round rain, it provides perfect conditions both for the lush natural vegetation and the intensive farming that has laid row upon dense row of narrow terraces across even the steepest hillsides. This is

Lions prowling through the golden savannah of the Masai Mara

Western Kenya

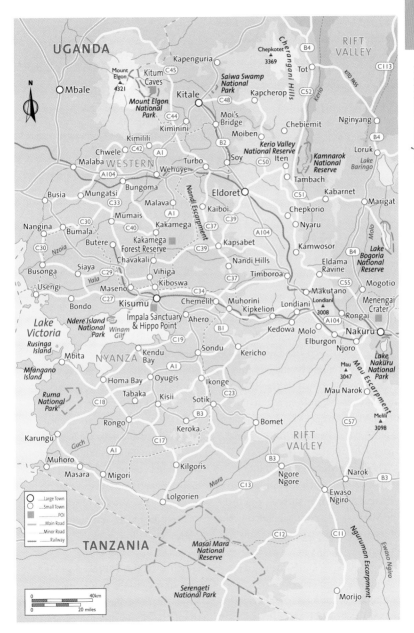

one of the most densely populated corners of the country, home to the Luo and Luyia, two of the largest tribes in Kenya, both of whom have a strong farming tradition.

Lake Victoria dominates the western fringe of the area, but there are many other attractions for the visitor, from the quite staggeringly vast tea plantations of Kericho to the Kakamega Forest Reserve, one of Kenya's last remaining areas of primeval forest and a birdwatcher's paradise. Beyond this, between Kitale and the Uganda border, rears the massive bulk of Mount Elgon, the country's second-highest mountain. If you wish to take full advantage of the area a 4WD vehicle is advisable.

THE MASAI MARA
The jewel in the crown

The Masai Mara is undoubtedly the jewel in Kenya's eco-holiday crown. Not only is it home to one of nature's most amazing animal spectacles, the annual Great Migration, but because of the Mara River's permanent water, it is also Kenya's best year-round game-viewing location.

The Masai Mara is divided into several sections, each administered in a different way. It may surprise you that the Mara is not a national park, in spite of its world importance. The main area is designated as the Masai Mara National Reserve, and is managed by two different authorities.

The Mara Conservancy manages the area west of the Mara River,

THE GREAT MIGRATION

Probably the most spectacular large mammal event on earth, the Great Migration is an annual movement of about 1.5 million wildebeest and 600,000 zebras, as they wend their way around an ecosystem in Tanzania and Kenya covering roughly 25,000sq km (9,653sq miles), in search of water and pasture.

Having calved in the southeast Serengeti in January and February, the wildebeest move north to better-watered pastures, arriving in the Masai Mara around the end of June and staying until about November.

During their migration the animals must cross the Mara River, which they sometimes do repeatedly, on each occasion risking their lives either to the enormous Mara River crocodiles, or to the real risk of drowning. As thousands of thrashing and panicking animals cross the river together, each year many are drowned.

Crossings occur only at a dozen or so regular points where the normally incised Mara River banks have been breached through years of animal migrations.

sometimes called the Mara Triangle, which is about a third of the whole. Narok County Council manages the section east of the river.

To the north and east of the National Reserve is an area referred to as the Mara Group Ranches. This is privately owned but communally run Maasai land, still part of the greater Mara ecosystem and also full of wildlife.

There are lodges and permanent camps in all three areas.

Getting to the Mara

The journey to the Masai Mara is spectacular whichever way you go, and should be viewed as an integral part of the whole experience. Scheduled flights by Safari Link and Air Kenya both leave from Wilson Airport. The route crosses first the Ngong Hills, made famous in *Out of Africa*, and then the Rift Valley, with views of the volcanoes Suswa and Longonot, before pushing south over the Masai steppe of southern Kenya.

By road the route heads over the Rift Valley Escarpment into the longest valley on the planet, passing between Suswa and Longonot, before climbing up the western escarpment towards Narok. There is then a choice of two new roads, each heading into the Mara via the Sekanani or Oloololo gates, one to the eastern end and the other to the west. During the rains the eastern route is normally preferred.

Your safari in the Mara

The first essential of your safari is a vehicle. During and after the rains, ensure your tour company uses only 4WD vehicles.

Next is the driver-guide, who will usually come with all the skills and knowledge to make your holiday a real success in many ways. Standards are normally high and an outstanding driver-guide will contribute enormously to the quality of your safari.

In the Mara you will usually stay in a permanent lodge such as Mara Serena or Keekorok, or if you want something slightly more traditional you can stay in a permanent tented camp such as Governors, Kichwa Tembo or Intrepids.

Hide at Keekorok Lodge, south-central Masai Mara

Wildlife is never far away in the Mara

Within the whole Mara ecosystem there are about 30 locations to choose from and, generally, standards are extremely high. Do not be put off by the idea of 'camping'. Each tent will be beautifully furnished and will come with its own en-suite bathroom, flush toilet and shower. Expect to be pampered.

Lodges and camps use both areas within the National Reserve and the Group Ranches for their game drives, depending on where the best animal viewing is to be found.

The game drive

Most safari holidays have two game drives per day, one in the early morning and a second in the late afternoon–early evening. Sometimes you may be away for a whole day and enjoy a picnic lunch.

Depending on where your lodge or camp is located, there will be local hotspots where game viewing is almost always good. The rivers always have animals needing to drink and there is usually something to see at the Musiara Swamp. Rivers which dry up, such as the Talek and Sand Rivers, will often have pools which become vital waterholes. These become a magnet not only for

SOME TIPS ON GAME VIEWING

- Don't crowd the animals with too many vehicles.
- Keep quiet near animals.
- Be patient. Maybe something is just about to happen, such as a river crossing.
- Remember that some animals, such as cheetahs, hunt during the day. Do not stop them from doing this.
- Keep to the tracks; there are enough in the Masai Mara already.
- Switch off the engine while taking photographs.
- Be courteous to other game viewers.

wildebeest, zebra and buffalo, but also, of course, for the Masai Mara's 500 or so lions.

During the migrations, your driver may automatically head for one of the well-known crossing points on the Mara River. If you are lucky with your timing, you may see Masai Mara's most spectacular event, a river crossing of thousands of migrating animals driven on by the need to reach the other side.

Wildebeest and zebra in a state of panic at the river

The scarlet warriors

A group of Maasai *moranis*

Closely related nomadic tribes, the Maasai and Samburu are herders of cattle and goats (many Samburu also keep camels). Physically beautiful, they dress in red, which signifies power and strength, blood and courage, along with a lot of intricate bead jewellery. They believe in one god, Ngai, but religion is a private affair, and the rites of passage, from the naming of a child to circumcision, are secular ceremonies. Their traditional diet is cow's blood and milk.

The *manyatta* is home to the extended family group, with the husband and each of his wives having separate houses. Girls stay with their mothers until they marry, boys move in with their fathers at about six. The small boys are in charge of the herds. After circumcision, at between 14 and 17, they become *moranis* (warriors), and move off to live in a separate village. Some traditional *morani* activities such as cattle-raiding and lion-hunting are now largely history. At about 25, the men become junior elders, and are allowed to marry. Their duties now are counting the herds out and in and decision-making. All the day-to-day work, including building houses, is done by the women, who traditionally have no rights or say in tribal affairs.

Immensely proud peoples, both tribes have preferred to retain their traditional lifestyle in the face of all odds and only very recently have any succumbed to Western ways or even been to school. Even so, they cling to polygamy, huge families and ever-growing herds, with cattle or camels the only symbol of wealth they recognise. The authorities are actively seeking to make them join the modern world. For the moment, they remain guardians of one of the last great nomadic traditions in Africa.

Today, many boys do not follow the traditional *morani* path, but go to secondary school and on to university. In the Masai Mara, 10 per cent of collected revenue goes towards Maasai communities, funding schools and clinics and supplying university fees, amongst other things.

The Maasai are scattered throughout southern and central Kenya and northern Tanzania, with a break in the Central Highlands, which is an area dominated by the Kikuyu. From Nairobi, one reaches Maasai lands at Ngong – about a 30-minute drive from the capital.

The most colourful, proud and famous of Kenya's many tribes, the Maasai live a largely traditional lifestyle

MOUNT ELGON AND ENVIRONS

The whole Mount Elgon area enjoys heavy rains almost every afternoon, so try to do your sightseeing and complete any journeys on dirt roads in the morning, before you become shrouded in cloud and the roads are rendered impassable.

Kakamega Forest Reserve

A 45sq km (17sq mile) forest reserve tucked beneath the Nandi Escarpment at around 1,500m (4,921ft), Kakamega is a throwback to the days when rainforest covered the wetter parts of central Africa. The only remaining section of such forest in Kenya, it has 125 species of massive hardwood trees and literally hundreds of species of birds and animals, many of which are found nowhere else in Kenya. Look out for the brilliantly coloured turacos, colobus and blue monkeys, the bush-tailed porcupine and the scaly-tailed flying squirrel.

Two access roads turn off the Kisumu–Kitale Rd (A1), about 10km (6 miles) south and 20km (12 miles) north of Kakamega respectively. There is a small rest house, 5km (3 miles) walk from the road at Shinalyu village. Take your own food. Free admission.

Kitale

A sleepy town with a population of about 30,000, Kitale houses the excellent **National Museum of Western Kenya**. It was founded in 1972 around the private collection of butterflies, medals and oddities of a local farmer, Colonel Stoneham. Other sections include animal, geological and ethnographic displays, such as a fascinating case on traditional medicines with treatments for bone cancer, nose bleeds and syphilis. Outside, a nature trail leads through a small area of forest and past some traditional homesteads, crocodile and tortoise pens.

Kisumu Rd. www.museums.or.ke. Open: daily 9.30am–6pm. Admission charge.

Mount Elgon National Park

This remote and beautiful park covers 169sq km (65sq miles) on the eastern slopes of Mount Elgon (the western slopes are in Uganda). A free-standing volcanic cone, the mountain is the second highest in Kenya, at 4,321m (14,177ft). When the weather is clear (in the mornings), the views from the mountain, even from the gate, are magnificent, while the higher slopes are swathed in dense forest, home to bushbuck, buffalo and elephant, as well as a host of smaller animals and birds. At the top there is moorland, with giant alpine vegetation (*see p9*). The actual summit consists of a ring of rocky peaks surrounding the crater lake.

About 9km (5½ miles) from the gate, eroded volcanic ash has formed a series of deep caves. The largest and most accessible (about 0.5km/⅓ mile walk from the road) are the **Kitum Caves**, said to have been the inspiration for H. Rider Haggard's novel *She*. The caves are natural salt licks and at night the elephants pick their way up precipitous mountain paths and across the unstable rock falls to gouge the minerals from the walls. It is possible to see the marks made by their tusks, as well as vast colonies of bats. Wear shoes with a good grip and take a powerful torch.

Tel: (054) 20329. The park gate is about 30km (19 miles) west of Kitale. Camping only within the park. Alternatively, stay at the simple lodge just outside, or Lokitela Farm about 18km (11 miles) away (www.bush-homes.co.ke). Open: daily 6am–6pm. You will need permission and a ranger with you if walking. Admission charge.

Saiwa Swamp National Park

This tiny 200ha (495-acre) park, in the swamplands surrounding the Koitobos River, was set up to preserve one of the few remaining natural habitats of the sitatunga antelope in Kenya. Access is on foot only, with a series of walking trails and observation points. There is excellent birdwatching and the remote prospect of seeing a leopard.

5km (3 miles) off the main road, 18km (11 miles) northeast of Kitale. Open: daily 6am–6pm. There are no facilities. Admission charge.

The sitatunga is found only at Saiwa Swamp and a few other locations

LAKE VICTORIA

*'. . . there lay the end of our pilgrimage –
a glistening bay of the great Lake
surrounded by low shores and shut in to
the south by several islands, the whole
softly veiled and rendered weirdly
indistinct by a dense haze. The view,
with arid-looking euphorbia-clad slopes
shading gently down to the muddy beach,
could not be called picturesque, though it
was certainly pleasing.'*

JOSEPH THOMSON
Through Maasai Land, 1883

At 67,483sq km (26,055sq miles), Lake
Victoria is the second-largest freshwater
lake in the world (only Lake Superior in
North America is larger). The first
European to sight this vast inland sea
was John Hanning Speke in 1858. On
little evidence and a strong instinct, he
declared the lake to be the source of the
White Nile, only to be derided by other
explorers. It was 1875 before HM
Stanley eventually proved him right.

From then on, the lake attracted
intense interest in Europe as the
colonial powers dreamed in vain of
opening up a navigable route along the
Nile to the Mediterranean. Their
attempts to reach Uganda across the
lake were also responsible for creating
the East African Railway and colonising
the Kenyan Highlands (*see pp142–3*).

Now officially renamed Nyanza
(a name rarely used), the lake acts as
a boundary between Tanzania, Uganda
and Kenya, which owns only a tiny
corner – 3,785sq km (1,461sq miles).
It is remarkable more for its sheer size
than its physical beauty, the persistent
haze and cloud cover turning its surface
a dull steely grey for much of the year.
Only a handful of fishing boats and one
local ferry (*see p136*) ever break the
monotony of the scene.

The Luo tribe fish for Nile perch and tilapia in Lake Victoria

Kisumu market is one of the largest, most varied and colourful in the country

Kisumu

The third-largest city in Kenya, with a population of about 160,000, Kisumu was founded in 1901 as the inland railhead of the East African Railway. At the time, it was named Port Florence after Florence Whitehouse, wife of the railway's chief engineer, who hammered the last rail into place.

Today, it is a friendly, bustling, rather old-fashioned centre with few actual sights. Take the time to wander around and visit the splendid market at the corner of Nairobi Road and Jomo Kenyatta Highway.

Kisumu Impala Sanctuary and Hippo Point

This 16ha (40-acre) game sanctuary and animal orphanage is one of the few homes of the rare sitatunga (antelope). **Hippo Point**, next door, is theoretically the best place for seeing hippos, but keep in mind they do wander. Both places are excellent spots from which to see Lake Victoria's spectacular sunsets.

Beside the Sunset Hotel, 3km (2 miles) south of Kisumu. www.kws.org. Both are open at all times. Admission charge. Check at the hotel about the area's security.

Kisumu Museum

An excellent small museum with some curious oddities, such as a stuffed lion savaging a stuffed wildebeest. Most of it is given over to a fascinating display of local traditional lifestyle and crafts, from musical instruments to a reconstructed Luo village. There is also an aquarium, a snake park and pit and a crocodile pool.

Nairobi Rd, 1.5km (1 mile) from the city centre. Tel: (035) 40804. www.museums.or.ke. Open: daily, 9.30am–6pm. Admission charge.

Ndunga Beach and Fishing Village

This small fishing village is an excellent place to see the traditional lifestyle of the lake fishermen. You can also hire a local fisherman and his canoe for a paddle through the nearby papyrus reed beds for a closer look at the hippos and the birds ranging from jacanas to pelicans. The afternoon, when the fleet is in, is the best time to go.

4km (2½ miles) west of the Sunset Hotel. The village is open daily 8am–6pm. Negotiable fees for photos and accompanied canoe trips.

Mfangano Island

There are some remote rock paintings and a small fishing community here, but the island has now been taken over as an upmarket fishing camp for anglers interested in Nile perch and tiger fish.
55km (34 miles) west of Homa Bay. The only local transport is a twice-weekly ferry from Homa Bay. Visitors to the camp fly in from the Masai Mara. Bookings via Governors Camp, PO Box 48217, Nairobi. Tel: (020) 273 4000. www.governorscamp.com

Ndere Island National Park

You can wander freely on foot on this tiny island game park (4.2sq km/ 1²/₃sq miles), which has snakes, hippos, crocodiles, sitatunga and several species of waterbird.

Hire a boat from the Kisumu Yacht Club (the round trip is about 6 hours, including time for a walk). Alternatively, drive to Kaloka Beach, Seme (40km/ 25 miles west of Kisumu) and hire a local canoe. There are no facilities. www.kws.org. Open: daily 6am–6pm. Admission charge.

Ruma National Park

A 120sq km (46sq mile) national park enclosing the Lambwe Valley, Ruma is 10km (6 miles) from the shore of Lake Victoria and boasts Kenya's only herd of roan antelope.
The gate is 32km (20 miles) southwest of Homa Bay. Tel: (0385) 22007. www.kws.org. Open: daily 6am–6pm. Admission charge.

Sunset over Lake Victoria from Rusinga Island

Fields under cultivation near Kericho

velvet which sprawls out from the town and over the hills for miles around. It seems to go on forever, punctuated only by the women in thick plastic aprons who force their way through the tightly planted bushes, throwing the shoots over their backs into great wicker baskets. It is hard to imagine there are enough people in the world to drink it all.

The tour is booked through the Kericho Tea Hotel (see p172) Tel: (052) 30004.

Rusinga Island

Here Mary Leakey found the skull of 3-million-year-old *Proconsul africanus*. Today, there is an exclusive fishing camp and the mausoleum of Tom Mboya (1930–69), a great nationalist leader, assassinated in Nairobi.

40km (25 miles) west of Homa Bay, along an appallingly rough road. The island is connected to the mainland by a causeway. Most people fly in from the Masai Mara. Rusinga Island Lodge. Tel: (020) 253 1314. www.rusinga.com

THE WESTERN HIGHLANDS
Kericho

Kericho itself is a small, pleasant, up-country town whose architecture and ambience has changed little in the last 30 years. The real reason for coming here is for the massive **tea plantation**, a veritable sea of neatly trimmed green

Tabaka

This small village is the home of all the pastel pink and white soapstone on sale in Kenya. Everyone in the village is involved in quarrying or carving, and every household has a small array of carvings laid out beside the front door. There have been quarries here since the 1920s, but there is no danger, as yet, of supplies running out. Three quarries are currently being worked, each employing up to 50 people. The carvers (all men) pay about 3,000 shillings for a lorry load of up to 8 tonnes of the stone – a three-month supply. Most can turn out between six and ten carvings a day, dependent on size. The women carry the sackloads of stone from the quarries to the co-operative office and give the pieces a final polish.

Turn left off the Homa Bay Rd 11km (7 miles) beyond Kisii. Tabaka village is 6km (4 miles) further on. The quarries, on the far side of the hill, work from Mon–Fri 8am–5pm. Continue on to Rongo and turn right to get back on to the main road.

The coast

A great sweep of palm-fringed silver sands, mangrove swamps and gentle turquoise creeks, Kenya's 480km (298-mile) coast gazes calmly out across the coral reefs to the open sea. It is hard to envisage it as a key to the great Indian Ocean trading routes. It seems too peaceful to have known the many bloody wars that have rocked its shores, as the great maritime powers of the world battled to gain control of its sheltered harbours.

Today Mombasa, built on a 15sq km (6sq mile) island surrounded by a superb natural harbour is still, quietly, a great trading centre, with a massive, modern port. Nearly three quarters of a million people call the city home. It has a large Asian population which retains its own culture and whose people are successful traders. The rest of the population forms a melting pot of tribes from all over Kenya and nearby regions. The original Swahili people in the city have long been absorbed into the mainstream, but those in the villages still live a traditional life as small-scale farmers and coastal fishermen. The whole region is strongly Islamic. Meanwhile, the coast has had a new incarnation as a popular holiday playground.

More and more resort hotels line the coast, but most, though large, are still low-key. People come here to snorkel on the reefs, for the deep-sea fishing and, above all, to relax under a tropical sun and the coconut palms on a beautiful and still relatively empty beach.

LAMU ARCHIPELAGO

Lamu is an enchanted archipelago of low coral islands, sand dunes and mangroves, calm creeks and sailing *dhows*, cut off from the mainland and the rest of the world. Lamu town, like so many of the towns along this coast, was a great Swahili trading centre, but its island fastness protected it from the ravages of the Portuguese and the Galla tribe, and here above all there is a continuity of history and architecture.

The area became notorious in the 1960s as one of the great hippy hang-outs, but in more recent years the locals reached breaking point and cleared the drugs and nudists from their beaches. In addition, the island's inaccessibility and the efforts of historians have, so far, combined to save the area from mass-market development. Tourism is important here, but it is small scale, designed for those who are willing to merge unobtrusively with the local lifestyle. There are no discos and little alcohol but the people are friendly, the

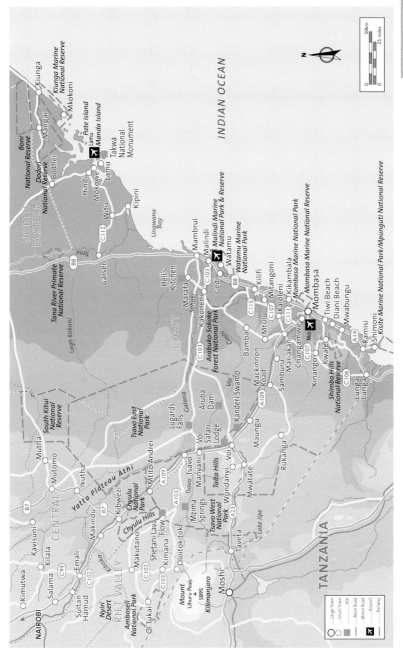

seafood is wonderful and the atmosphere so laid back it's horizontal.
(*See* Lamu town walk, *pp96–7.*)

Manda Island

Home of the airport, Manda Island is the gateway to Lamu. It also has wonderful beaches, a line of coral reef running along the western shore, a large creek, thickly hung with mangroves and the ruins of Takwa, a religious site abandoned in the 18th century.
Directly across the channel from Lamu town (see Boat tour, pp98–9).

Matondoni

A small village on the west of Lamu Island, Matondoni has long been famous as a *dhow*-building centre. It is possible to wander through the yards, watching the villagers at work building or repairing the boats.
2 hours by foot or dhow *from Lamu town.*

Pate Island

This remote island has three historic towns – Pate, Siyu and Faza. This was, and is, the other main population centre in the Lamu archipelago, but after centuries of in-fighting, Lamu won a decisive victory when it massacred the Pate fleet at Shela in 1812. Since then, Pate has been sliding inexorably into decay.

Probably founded in the 14th century, **Pate town** has some old but poorly maintained Swahili houses. Nearby are the overgrown ruins of the original 13th-century **Nabahani** settlement. In the centre of the island, **Siyu** was founded

Lamu's famous sand dunes

The waterfront at Shela

in the 15th century, and between the 17th and 18th centuries became a major centre of Islamic studies. Now much smaller, it still retains a formidable fort dating from the 19th century.

Directly south of Siyu, the ruined city of **Shanga** was built in the 10th century and abandoned in the 14th. **Faza**, on the north coast, is now the provincial government headquarters. It is an old settlement, but has been destroyed so many times that the vast majority of its buildings are modern. *19km (12 miles) northeast of Lamu town. Access by* dhow *or local motor launch, then on foot. You will need to spend the night on the island, so be prepared to camp or stay with a local family.*

Shela

This is the nearest village to Lamu town and is at the start of a spectacular 11km (7-mile) long beach. Although an ancient settlement, it has few old buildings other than the 1829 **Juma'a Mosque**, and is best known now as the island's upmarket resort.

Shela village is a 45-minute walk from Lamu town; the beach stretches out beyond that.
(*See also* Boat tour, *pp98–9.*)

- Almost everyone flies to Lamu, with scheduled services from Nairobi, Mombasa and Malindi.
- Local transport is mostly by *dhow* or, for transfers, fast motorboats. If you wish to explore the islands, you will need to walk. Donkeys are widely used for carrying goods.
- Remember to be sensitive to Muslim culture and to Kenyan law. No nude or topless bathing and no swimwear away from the beach.
- Remember that alcoholic drinks will normally only be available in resort hotels.

Walk: Lamu town

Lamu dates from 1350, but was built on an earlier 9th-century site. The whole town has been designated a UNESCO World Heritage Site, attracting global funding for the careful restoration of the old, roughly cut, coral-rag houses. This walk takes you through the narrow streets and alleys to Lamu's most fascinating sights.

Allow 30 minutes' walking time and 3 to 4 hours for sightseeing. The sights are shown on the map on p98.

Start at the main jetty.

The seafront

Lamu seafront is a fascinating mix of *dhows* and donkeys, and for the Lamu folk this is the centre of the universe. The men are wrapped in their colourful *kikois* (sarongs) and many of the women are fully veiled in black *buibui*. People are almost universally friendly and, in spite of all the quayside activity, you realise that this is a place where you can slow down for a while.
Walk towards the old jetty.

Petley's Inn

This old colonial hotel, founded by Percy Petley, was famous for its discomfort in the 1930s, when visitors often had to cook their own food and claimed that the rats of Lamu were big enough to eat the cats – of which there are still many! The hotel is better now, and its upstairs bar is one of the few places in town to serve alcohol.

Lamu Museum

Directly opposite the old jetty, this is the old British District Commissioner's house with magnificent carved doors, flanked by cannons used by the British to bombard the Sultan of Witu in 1892. The museum is excellent, offering a detailed history of the town and region.
Walk west along the harbourfront to the donkey sanctuary (about 100m/110yds).

Donkey Sanctuary

A small sanctuary set up by a British foundation which rescues badly treated donkeys, who live out their days in comfort here.
Turn left up the narrow alley beside the sanctuary and follow the signs through the web of tiny back streets to the Swahili House Museum.

Swahili House Museum

The smaller, inner courtyard of this 18th-century house is surrounded by open rooms decorated with carved plaster niches for the porcelain collection and furnished in traditional Swahili style. Fish were kept in the water tank to eat mosquito larvae. Look out for the pasta machine in the upstairs kitchen.

Retrace your steps down through the alleys and turn right on to the main street, one block back from the seafront.

Main Street

Originally Lamu's seafront, this stretch is now the town's main shopping street, a warren of shaded little shops and cafés. Go back to browse in the early evening when snacks are roasting over open braziers and the woodcarvers are sitting working in their doorways.

Walk along the street to the square in front of the fort, at the far end.

Lamu Fort

Built by the Omanis between 1810 and 1821, this massive fort became the town prison from 1910 to 1984. It now houses a splendid walk-through aquarium and natural history museum. The square around the fort is home to a busy, colourful morning market.

Turn back towards the seafront and walk along to the starting point.

Lamu Museum and the Swahili House Museum are both open daily, 9.30am–6pm. www.museums.or.ke. Admission charge.
Lamu Fort is now open to the public, daily 8am–6pm. Admission charge during exhibition times.

Dhows on Lamu's seafront

Boat tour: Manda's mangroves

This is a blueprint for the ultimate lazy day, with a little sightseeing, a little sunbathing and a little sailing. Take a hat and sunblock as you can get badly burnt on the water.

Those in a hurry could cram it into half a day.

Hire a dhow from the main jetty in Lamu town.

1 The *dhows*

Unlike the large trading *dhows*, these are small boats of 6 to 8m (20–26ft),

similar in design to those used by fishermen here for 1,000 years. They normally have a crew of two; one on the tiller and one to handle the sails. *Sail south along the coast, with excellent views of the Lamu town seafront to Shela.*

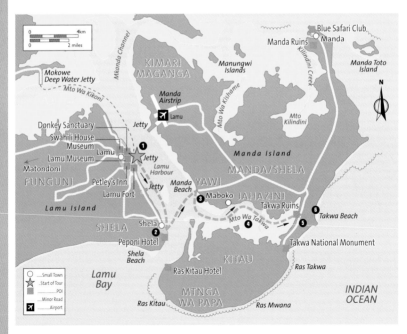

2 Shela

Lamu town's nearest neighbour, Shela, is a delightful waterfront Swahili village. The coast nearest Lamu is lined with *dhows*, but round the corner, beyond Peponi Hotel, is one of Kenya's longest and most idyllic beaches. Spend the morning basking in the sun and then head towards **Peponi**'s, the best hotel in the vicinity, for a gourmet lunch.

3 Fresh fish and an open fire

As an alternative, spend the morning fishing off the *dhow*, and land on deserted **Manda Beach**, directly opposite Shela, for a swim and to barbecue your catch. Arrange this with the boatmen the day before and they will provide the extras, such as bread, salad and fruit.

4 The mangrove swamps

From Manda Beach, you sail round into the wide creek which almost splits the island in half. On your left is **Maboko**, a coral-mining village which is the only permanent settlement left on Manda. Most people left the island when the fresh water ran out, and the villagers have to import their water from Lamu. As the creek narrows to a watery green tangle of mangrove swamp, it also gets shallower.

5 Takwa ruins

The Muslim town of Takwa flourished in the 16th and 17th centuries, and is thought to have been founded by people fleeing from warfare on the mainland.

Ocean-going *dhows* were the main trading transport for 1,000 years

Strategically situated out of sight of the sea, behind the dunes, it was surrounded by a 2m (6½ft) high wall. There are 110 known coral-rag houses and stores, all in ruins, but there were also many humbler houses of mud and thatch. In addition, there is a mosque and a fine pillar tomb dated AH 1094 (1683). Takwa is only accessible on the rising tide, so the timetable of this tour needs to take account of tide times, which change daily.

www.museums.or.ke. Open: daily 9.30am–6pm. Admission charge.

6 Takwa Beach

A footpath leads across the dunes to Takwa Beach. Open to the ocean through a gap in the reef, this stretch of shore is subject to large breakers and a strong undertow. **Manda Toto Island**, to the north, has some of the finest coral in the Lamu archipelago.

Sail gently home as the sunset lights up the Lamu skyline and the wail of the muezzin reaches out across the water.

MALINDI

As leader of one of the greatest and friendliest of the medieval city-states along the Kenya coast, the king of Malindi opened up diplomatic relations with China during the voyage of the great explorer Zheng He, in 1414. He sent a present of a giraffe, an oryx and a zebra to the Chinese court and the giraffe was so well received that it became the Chinese symbol of Perfect Virtue, Perfect Government and Perfect Harmony. A later king of Malindi was also the first to offer the hand of friendship to Vasco da Gama, in 1498. When the explorer returned the following year, the first Portuguese trading post was set up here and the doors of East Africa were opened to Europe.

Today, Malindi is a busy coastal town with a strong tourist element along the beach. There is a high proportion of Italians in the resident population. It has numerous hotels and several restaurants and discos, but daytime activities are clearly focused on the sea. Its beaches are excellent, with none of the seaweed that plagues those further south, and the coral reefs are very accessible – you can even walk to some at low tide. There is brilliant diving and snorkelling although some of the coral itself has been badly damaged by careless flippers. Malindi and Watamu are also Kenya's main centres for deep-sea fishing, made popular, like so many other places, by that obsessively macho sportsman Ernest Hemingway.

Malindi has lots of self-catering accommodation, and generally speaking, one can usually just turn up and be sure to find somewhere nice at a very reasonable price.

120km (75 miles) north of Mombasa. There is an airport 2km (1¹/₄ miles) south of the town and a small tourist office on the Lamu Rd. Tel: (042) 20747.

The Vasco da Gama cross, set up to commemorate the explorer's visit to Malindi

The Crocodile Paradise

A small but attractive park with the usual array of giant tortoises and terrapins, snakes (from cobras and mambas to pythons) and crocodiles. The tour guides are more enthusiastic than knowledgeable and are eager for you to handle some of the livestock, under supervision, including baby crocodiles and terrapins and a very large python.

About 5km (3 miles) south of the town, near the entrance to the Malindi Marine National Park. Open: daily 9am–5.30pm; feeding at 4pm on Wed & Fri. Admission charge.

The Town House beach bar, Malindi

Juma'a Mosque

The largest of Malindi's 12 mosques, this is a modern building on the site of the old slave market. Among the graves beside it is a 15th-century pillar tomb belonging to Sheikh Abdul Hassan.

In the heart of the old town, near the beach.

Malindi Marine National Park

This 6sq km (2sq mile) national park, together with the surrounding 213sq km (82sq mile) reserve and the Watamu National Marine Park (*see p103*) make up a biosphere reserve that takes in a 30km (19-mile) long stretch of coast, including the shore, with its mix of mangroves, casuarina trees, sea grass beds and the coral reef.

Most of the hotels run boat excursions to the coral reef, but the park entrance and the mass of small boats for hire are about 6km (4 miles) south of the town, at the

end of the hotel strip. Tel: (042) 20845. www.kws.org. Open: daily 7am–7pm. Admission charge.

Portuguese Church

Built in the early 16th century and surrounded by the old Malindi cemetery, this tiny, square, whitewashed chapel is thought to have been the first Christian church in East Africa. In 1542, St Francis Xavier buried two soldiers here during his journey to India. Inside is a faint mural of the Crucifixion.

The southern end of the beach road. The church is managed by the Museums of Kenya.

Vasco da Gama cross

In 1499, Vasco da Gama erected a simple cross made of Lisbon stone on a coral rag base at the entrance to the bay. The cross itself is original, but the base is a 16th-century replacement, later concreted into position.

On a rocky headland at the southern end of the bay. Access across the bay or via a footpath off the beach road.

The coast

MALINDI ENVIRONS
Arabuko-Sokoke Forest National Park

A 417sq km (161sq mile) forest reserve, Arabuko-Sokoke protects one of the last large stretches of dense, ancient coastal forest in Kenya. With numerous rare trees, plants and butterflies, it is also a haven for a variety of endangered creatures such as the grey-white Sokoke scops owl, the Zanzibar sombre greenbul, the 35cm (14in) high Ader's duiker and the yellow-rumped elephant shrew.

The forest stretches south from Gedi to Kilifi. Tel: (042) 32462. www.kws.org. Open to the public with permission from the forestry department. Admission charge.

Gedi

This 18ha (44-acre) ruined city flourished from the 13th to early 17th centuries. Archaeological finds, ranging from Ming porcelain and Persian glazed ware to a Venetian bead, make it clear that this was a comfortable, if not rich,

Arabuko-Sokoke Forest – there is little forest like this left at the coast

trading port (the sea has now retreated about 5km/3 miles).

Gedi was destroyed twice; the first time probably by Mombasa in about 1530, the second by the Galla tribe 200 years later (*see p123*). Its name means 'precious' in Galla, but the town was never of great importance, and is not mentioned in early travellers' accounts of the coast.

The ruins have long been swallowed up by the forest, with the coral walls set in deep green, dappled glades surrounded by baobab trees hung with lianas. It is a wonderfully atmospheric place at the centre of numerous local superstitions and ghost stories. The excavated section, just inside the northern stretch of the double ring of city walls, must have been the wealthy part of town because it contains the 15th- and 16th-century Great Mosque and Palace. Next to these is a tight web of 14 stone-built houses, such as the House of the Ivory Box and the House of the Chinese Cash, named by romantic archaeologists after the treasures found inside them. Also in this area are several pillar tombs, including the Dated Tomb with the Arabic date AH 802 (1399) inscribed on it. Nearby, the Tomb of the Fluted Pillar marks a pathway to the House of the Dhow (with a *dhow* etched into an inside wall). Many of the living areas have deep wells and sophisticated toilets that are a major source of fascination.

A small museum contains many of the finds, which range from pottery

Sunset over the mangrove swamps of Mida Creek, near Watamu

jars to personal possessions such as an iron lamp, scissors and a bronze eye pencil. Just outside the historic site is a reconstructed Giriama folk village.

Many of the forest creatures from Arabuko-Sokoke can also be found on the forest trails around Gedi. Watch out for giant land snails, giant millepedes and black mambas!

1.5km (1 mile) off the main Mombasa Rd, 16km (10 miles) south of Malindi. Open: daily 7am–6pm. Admission charge. There is an excellent guidebook and site plan on sale at the ticket office.

Watamu
Watamu Marine National Park
This 10sq km (4sq miles) national park, with great possibilities for diving and snorkelling, is the most obvious attraction. It is one of the finest such parks in Kenya, a dazzling playground for fish and sea creatures of every hue, where fish come to tap on your goggles and urchins wave as you pass. However, Watamu is equally important as one of the world's great deep-sea big-game

fishing locations. A veritable armada of high-tech fishing boats, all bristling with the latest gear, rides at anchor just off the main resorts.

Just south of Watamu beach, **Mida Creek** is a large area of tidal mudflats, mangrove swamps and reeds that offer perfect conditions for many wading birds, such as stints, sandpipers and plovers. Between March and May and August to October, the permanent residents are joined by great flocks of migrants. Many birds that breed in Europe spend the winter here. Near the creek, the underwater **Tewa Caves** are the breeding ground for a colony of gentle-giant rock cod, up to 400kg (882lb) and 2m (6½ft) long, which will feed from the hands of divers.

About 23km (14 miles) south of Malindi, off the main Mombasa Rd. Most of the hotels offer trips in glass-bottomed boats, snorkelling and diving. Alternatively, you can hire a boat from the beach or at the entrance to the park, just south of the Turtle Bay Hotel. Admission charge.

MOMBASA

A thousand years ago, when many Western cities were little more than muddy villages, Mombasa was a sophisticated city. By the 15th century, it was trading regularly with Persia, China and India and its merchants were said to be so rich they wore cloth made of gold.

The end of that century, however, spelt the end of the golden age. In 1498, Vasco da Gama arrived and although he found the town hostile, it was a rich prize and the Portuguese sacked Mombasa four times over the next 90 years. Meanwhile, a new enemy, the ferocious Zimba tribe, was sweeping down the coast, burning and destroying. By 1589, Mombasa was too weak to fight back and the city finally fell to the Portuguese. Plagued by disease and warfare, they remained in control until 1697, when a prolonged Omani siege drove them out. There was one last hiccup of Portuguese rule, from 1728 to 1729, but Mombasa soon reverted to the Arabs.

In 1741, the local hereditary governors, the Mazruis, broke away to create an independent state. Battling constantly against the Omanis, in 1824 they called in the British to establish a protectorate but this lasted only until 1826. In 1837, the city fell, the Mazruis were exiled and the state once again became part of the Omani Sultanate of Zanzibar.

Meanwhile, commercial Mombasa was growing fat again, this time on the profits of the slave trade. As British interest in the region grew, it became the base for the exploration of the hinterland, and in 1888, the Imperial British East Africa Company set up its headquarters here. In 1895, the British leased a stretch of the coast from the Sultan of Zanzibar and Mombasa came under British rule. It still officially belonged to Zanzibar until ceded to independent Kenya in 1963.

Today, built on a 15sq km (6sq mile) island surrounded by a superb natural harbour, the city, Kenya's second largest, is still one of Africa's major ports with a population of nearly three quarters of a million. The harbour itself has been transformed into a modern container port and there has been a massive proliferation of tourist resorts, some of them very luxurious, on the mainland coasts to the north and south.

Mombasa has lost much of its status since the capital moved to Nairobi, however, and although it is noisy and colourful, it is an old-fashioned city whose colonial buildings retain a rather charming air of decaying splendour.

Fort Jesus

In 1593, the Portuguese began work on a fortified stronghold at the entrance of Mombasa Harbour, allowing access for supplies even during a siege. Designed and built by Portuguese architect João Batista Cairato, Fort Jesus covers about 1ha (2½ acres) and is roughly rectangular, with bastions at each

Mombasa Island

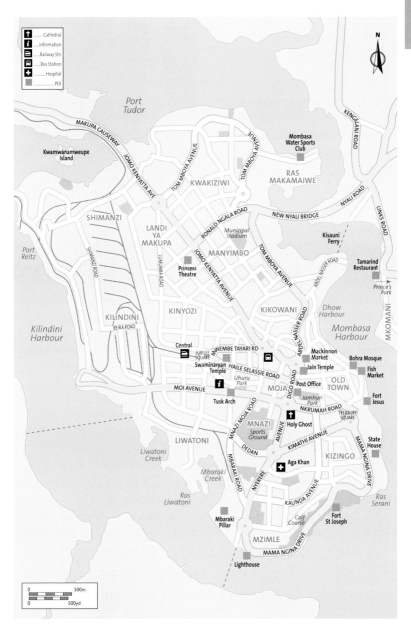

corner and in the centre of the seawall. The coral walls are about 2.5m (8ft) wide and 13m (43ft) high, with a walkway and gun emplacements round the top. The surrounding ditch varies in width from 3m to 12m (10–39ft). There have been many alterations and additions, both by later Portuguese commanders and by the Omanis.

In 1631–32, the fort was occupied during a local Arab revolt. From 1696 to 1698 it was the focus of a great siege by Omani Arabs which eventually broke the Portuguese rule of the coast. In 1895 it became the local prison. Since 1958 it has been a national monument.

The small museum houses an interesting ceramics collection and the finds from a Portuguese frigate wrecked here in 1697. The 18th-century Omani House, on the Bastion of Santo António, has displays on Swahili life and fabulous views over the Old Town. The Captain's Quarters, in the sea wall, were later transformed into a Mazrui audience hall. The graffiti here includes a eulogy to a Mazrui governor who went to Mecca in 1793.

Next to this, steps lead down to the sea. In the centre of the fort are the remains of several barracks blocks, the old church, a water cistern and a well.

Nkrumah Rd, beside the Old Town. Tel: (041) 312 839. www.museums.or.ke. Open: daily 9.30am–6pm. Admission charge. An excellent detailed guidebook is on sale at the ticket office.

Cannons still line the battlements of Mombasa's formidable Fort Jesus

Kilindini

Kilindini is the commercial port. Though not much of a tourist attraction, it is the main port of Kenya and also of Uganda and countries in central Africa.

Crossing the harbour entrance is the Likoni Ferry, which links Mombasa with the resort of Diani Beach.

Mama Ngina Drive

The drive runs along the southern end of the island, and is home to the Golf Club, Mombasa's casinos, the lighthouse and the State House, the residence of the president when he visits the coast.

The drive leads around the southeastern edge of the island from the Likoni ferry port to Treasury Square.

Modern city centre

The heart of modern Mombasa is tiny, a cross of four busy roads; Moi Avenue,

Nyerere Avenue, Nkrumah Road and Digo Road. The most interesting is **Moi Avenue**, which is lined by a double row of souvenir shops and stalls. It contains the city's most famous landmark, two pairs of crossed tusks, created as a triumphal arch to celebrate the coronation of Queen Elizabeth II, in 1953. Just round the corner, on Nyerere Road, is the stolid, Neo-Gothic **Holy Ghost Catholic Cathedral**.

Mombasa Old Town

Although people have lived here since the 2nd century AD, virtually nothing remains of the pre-19th-century city. Nevertheless, many of the older houses in the district were modelled on ancient Swahili designs and reused older doors and screens. The focus of the city has shifted to later developed areas and left this as a fascinating backwater of narrow and dark streets and crumbling warehouses.

Off Nkrumah Rd, near Fort Jesus (see Mombasa Old Town walk, pp108–9).

Treasury Square

A charming garden square surrounded by old colonial buildings, this is still the administrative centre of Mombasa. The old black and white Treasury Building of 1905 is now the District Administrative Headquarters, while the cream and white building next door is the Town Hall. In the park there is a monument to Allidina Isram, one of the leading Indian pioneers of colonial Kenya.

Between Mama Ngina Drive and Nkrumah Rd, near Fort Jesus.

Old Mombasa is still a living community although it has become one of the city's poorer areas

Walk: Mombasa Old Town

This is a gentle stroll through the narrow streets of the Old Town. Look for the charming details on the early houses, such as ornately carved doorways and balconies.

Allow 30 minutes plus shopping time. Take sensible security precautions. Avoid taking valuables with you.

Start from Fort Jesus (see pp104, 106). There is an excellent small guide to the Old Town on sale at the Fort.

1 Ali's Curio Market

Directly opposite Fort Jesus, Ali's Curio Market is one of the friendliest shopping stops in Mombasa. The building was originally constructed in 1898 as the Mombasa Police Station. *Walk past the shop to the right on to Mbarak Hinawy Rd.*

2 Mbarak Hinawy Road

Once named after Vasco da Gama, this was the route of the hand-pushed trolley buses which were the main public transport system from 1890 to 1923. The road is now named after Sir Mbarak Hinawy, the Sultan of Zanzibar's representative in Mombasa from 1931 to 1959. It has several interesting old houses, such as **Anil's Arcade** (No. 3), a three-storey house with tiered balconies. Numbers 5 and 9 have some fine Indian plasterwork

decoration. Number 10 is the **Mandhry Mosque**, founded in 1570 and the town's oldest mosque still in use. The well opposite is used for ritual ablutions. *Continue on and you come out into Government Square, beside the old dhow harbour.*

3 Government Square

This was the real hub of old Mombasa. On your left as you enter, the souvenir shop is the old Post Office, built in 1899 so that Indian railway workers could send money home to their families. At the back of the square is the morning fish market.

4 The old *dhow* harbour

The old Customs House stands beside the *dhow* harbour. Until Kilindini was founded in 1896, this was the main harbour for East Africa north of Zanzibar, handling hundreds of trading ships. *Dhows* stayed here for months, waiting for the seasonal reversal of trade winds to blow them back to the gulf.

At the far end of Government Square, walk along Bachuma Rd and turn right on to Ndia Kuu. A bit further along, a narrow passage beside a big yellow building dating from 1906 leads down to the Leven Steps.

5 The Leven Steps

Named after his ship, HMS *Leven*, these steps were built by a British naval lieutenant, James Emery, who briefly served as governor of Mombasa from 1824 to 1826. Today, the steps offer a peaceful viewpoint over the old harbour and across the bay to Nyali. *Return to Ndia Kuu and turn right.*

The site of the town's old North Gate is quickly reached. A side alley leads to the huge new Aga Khan Mosque. Turn back and retrace your steps along Ndia Kuu.

6 Ndia Kuu

Known by the Portuguese as the *Raposeira* (Foxhole), the modern name simply means Main Street. There are numerous fine old houses along here with ornately carved doorways, overhanging balconies and even open staircases. Among the finest are Numbers 28, 33 and 34.
Ndia Kuu leads straight back to Fort Jesus.

Walk: Mombasa Old Town

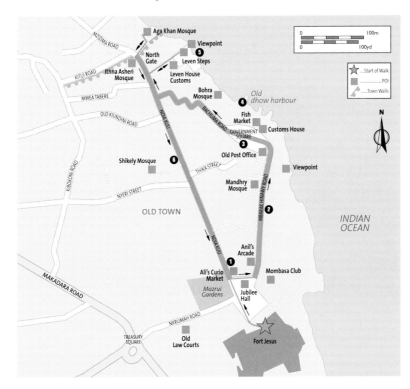

NORTH OF MOMBASA
Kilifi

This small town has become a popular centre for watersports and retirement homes for many white Kenyans. The rich blue, 15km (9 mile) long **Kilifi Creek** is a fine natural harbour and one of the most beautiful spots along the coast. Recently adorned by an elegant Japanese bridge, it often houses smart yachts as well as local fishing boats. Kilifi is also the major centre of the Giriama tribe, a Bantu people renowned as sorcerors and for their dance. The mangrove swamps inland are home to vast flocks of brilliant carmine bee-eaters.
54km (34 miles) northeast of Mombasa.

The mosque at the heart of the Mnarani ruins

Mnarani ruins

The ruined Swahili town of Mnarani is situated in a glorious setting overlooking Kilifi Creek. Destroyed in the 17th century by Galla tribes rampaging south from Somalia, the town lay undiscovered for nearly 400 years. Among the ruins are several pillar tombs and a mosque with some fine, fragmentary carvings from the Koran.
South side of Kilifi Creek. www.museums.or.ke. Open: daily 9.30am–6pm. Admission charge.

Mombasa Marine National Park

An area of 10sq km (4sq miles) surrounded by a further 200sq km (77sq mile) reserve, this is one of the most accessible of the line of marine parks that have been set up along the coast to preserve the fragile coral reef. There has been some damage to the coral and the quality here is not quite as good as in some of the less popular parks. Nevertheless, it offers some wonderful opportunities for diving and snorkelling amid a fantastic array of multicoloured fish.
Just off the Nyali headland, north of Mombasa, the park can be accessed by boat at any time. Tel: (041) 312 744. Admission charge.

Mtwapa Creek
Jumba La Mtwana

One of the chain of Swahili towns which flourished along the coast until it was abandoned in the 16th century. No one is sure why it was destroyed; it

could have been the result of a war between the Swahili city-states or one of the earliest incursions of the Somali tribes which eventually spelt the end of Gedi and Mnarani. It is a fairly small town, surrounded by baobabs, with the ruins of four mosques, a cemetery and numerous houses. From its name, which means 'House of Slaves', it is clear that this was a major slaving centre as well as trading in goods ranging from ivory to ambergris. There is a small beach set among the mangrove swamps.
16km (10 miles) north of the Mtwapa Creek bridge, signposted off the main Mombasa–Malindi Rd.
www.museums.or.ke. Open: daily 9.30am–6pm. Admission charge.

Kenya Marineland

The largest aquarium and snake park in the area, Kenya Marineland has the normal array of tortoises and turtles, crocodiles and snakes, but also houses the more lethal inhabitants of Kenya's waters, such as sharks and stingrays. The Marineland organises African entertainment.
1.5km (1 mile) off the main Mombasa–Malindi Rd. Tel: (041) 485 248. The turn-off is clearly signposted just north of the Mtwapa Creek bridge. Open: daily 8.30am–6pm. Admission charge.

Nyali

Stretching from Tudor Creek to Mtwapa Creek, just north of Mombasa Island, Nyali was the first area of the coast to be developed for tourism and

Mombasa environs

One of Tamarind's romantic floating restaurants

today has the widest selection of resorts and other attractions in the region.

Haller Park – formerly Bamburi Quarry Nature Trail

In 1971, agronomist Rene Haller began his rehabilitation of this once vast, ugly quarry. The result is an unmitigated success story – a delightful, shady complex covering more than 2sq km (^{3}/₄sq mile). It is at once a wildlife sanctuary, an award-winning conservation centre and a working organic farm that produces everything from fish and crocodiles to coconuts and timber. It has also become one of the main tourist attractions on the coast. Feeding time is at 4pm.
10km (6 miles) north of Mombasa on the main Malindi Rd. Tel: (041) 548 5901. www.lafargeecosystems.com. Open: daily 2–5pm. Admission charge. See also walk, pp114–15.

Mamba Village

This is one of the largest crocodile farms in Africa, with over 10,000 inmates. The pens are set in magnificent botanic gardens, which include a fine orchid collection and an alarming spiders' corner. There is a small aquarium with beautifully designed tanks and both horses and camels are available for rides. Other facilities include a bar, a restaurant and a disco. The crocodile feeding time is at 5pm.
Opposite the Nyali Golf Club on Links Rd, about 7km (4 miles) north of Mombasa. Tel: (041) 472 709. Open daily 8.30am–5.30pm. Admission charge.

Tamarind

Tamarind is the best-known restaurant on the Kenya coast, and has been elevated to an iconic, essential-visit status. Perched on the edge of a cliff above Mombasa Creek, it enjoys a classical view of the skyline of Old Mombasa. In the creek below are the two Tamarind Dhows, floating restaurants, ready to sail serenely around the island.

Nyali. Tel: (041) 474 600.
www.tamarind.co.ke,
www.tamarinddhow.com

Wild Waters

The Nyali waterslides are the nearest you get in Africa to a piece of Disneyland or Alton Towers. As a change from snorkelling and diving, children will love the collection of slides, pools and the rain-dance disco.

Links Rd, next to Mamba Village.
Tel: (041) 470 408.
www.wildwaterskenya.com

Takaungu

The oldest slaving port on the Kenya coast, Takaungu is now a charming Swahili village, strung out along a twisting turquoise creek overhung by wooded cliffs, and best known for its ornate woodcarving. At the centre of the village is the tomb of the last Mazrui sultan of Mombasa, who was overthrown and exiled to Takaungu in 1837.

Nearby, steps lead down to the creek which is used as the local laundry and pool. At the far end of the village, a footpath leads to a small but delightful beach.

Turn off the Mombasa–Malindi Rd,
10km (6 miles) south of Kilifi and follow
the dirt road for a further 5km (3 miles).

Waiting for tourists on Diani Beach

Walk: Haller Park, formerly Bamburi Quarry Nature Trail

Bamburi is a world-renowned example of conservation in action. A former coral quarry has been transformed into a tropical paradise with a whole series of self-sustaining ecosystems. All walks are guided, so no route has been given (see also p112).

Allow 2 hours.

For those arriving on foot from Nyali, or by public transport from Mombasa, 10km (6 miles) to the south, there is a small entrance beside the main road. If you have a car, continue a little further north, through the main entrance of the Portland Cement Factory.

Reception area and tortoise lawn

The reception area and ticket office, the real starting point of the tour, is surrounded by smooth grassy slopes, bordered by small lakes and ponds. The lawns are carefully cropped by giant Aldabra tortoises, some over 100 years old, which are happy to stop munching for long enough to have their necks scratched and photographs taken. There is also a picnic site, a refreshment stand and a lunchtime-only game restaurant here.

Game Sanctuary

A short distance on, there is an open fenced area surrounding a small lake. The water is planted with Nile cabbage, an efficient water filter which is harvested as livestock fodder and as a fertiliser. The sanctuary houses many species of wild animal, including hippos, buffalo, zebra, waterbuck, oryx, eland and rare Rothschild giraffes. There are also some 160 recorded species of birds.

Baobab Farm

Just west of the sanctuary is the working heart of the quarry, Baobab Farm, an ingenious integrated system of ecological farming. The intensive fish farm produces 11 different species of tilapia for sale. Any leftovers are fed to the crocodiles in the neighbouring pen. Some of the crocodiles are released back into the wild; others are farmed for their meat and skins. The dirty water from the crocodile pens and the fish farm is used to create and fertilise the rice paddies next door. The paddies filter the water which is then pumped back up to be reused in the fish farm.

Forestry area

Directly north of the sanctuary, this area was initially planted with trees that were able to survive on poor, salty rock, such as the Australian casuarina. A colony of giant millipedes was introduced to help them create humus. As the soil has improved and the trees have matured, the crop has been harvested for use in construction and as firewood. The area is now being replanted with a variety of over 150 local species, including hardwoods and coconuts. Serval cats and porcupines live in pens under the trees, while Vervet, Sykes' and Mona monkeys play in the branches above.

The nurseries

North of the forest area, near the road gate, is an area of mangrove swamp and another working section of the farm that includes the fish and crocodile breeding pens, the fisheries research centre and the plant nursery.

The Snake Park

Back beside the reception area, a separate entrance leads into the small, walled snake park, with a wide variety of species, many of which have been collected within the quarry itself. The authorities say they prefer to have their snakes safely away from visitors' feet!

Hippos grazing in the ecologically friendly Haller Park

Walk: Haller Park, formerly Bamburi Quarry Nature Trail

SOUTH OF MOMBASA

The south coast was once remote territory, completely covered by the rich primeval Jadini Forest, of which only a few tiny fragments now remain. The area was notorious for its slaving activities and later for its huge coconut and sugar plantations, but the development of Diani Beach has brought it into the mainstream of Kenya's tourist industry. In the rarely visited far south there are some of the coast's finest coral reefs and deep-sea fishing grounds. There is a good road all the way, reached via the Likoni Ferry from the south end of Mombasa Island.

Diani Beach

Over 10km (6 miles) long and fringed with coconut palms, this stretch of dazzling white sand is a picturebook version of the perfect tropical beach. As a result, it has drawn developers like flies and is now covered by wall to wall resorts. They all have large grounds and, effectively, private beaches. Most of the hotels provide watersports, boat trips out to the coral reef, and some evening entertainment. Many tourists punctuate their stay at the coast with a short safari to Shimba Hills, Tsavo and Amboseli national parks.

At the far north of the beach on the Mwachema Estuary, next to the Indian Ocean Beach Lodge, stands the well-preserved 15th-century **Mwana Mosque**. On the southern section, opposite the track leading to the Trade Winds Hotel, stands a giant baobab,

so big it has been protected by presidential decree.

40km (25 miles) south of Mombasa. The access road links to the beach road at the centre of the hotel strip. Consult the forest of signs about which way to turn. It is not safe to walk around at night.

Msambweni

An isolated and, until recently, neglected fishing village in lovely surroundings, Msambweni is only visited by those looking to get away from it all. Meaning 'Place of the Antelope', it is another of the many old slaving towns along this coast and still has the remains of a 17th-century slave pen. The energetic can scramble over the coral outcrops along the beach and, at low tide further down the coast, walk across to **Funzi Island**. This small island recently joined the tourist beat

Quiet, tree-lined Shimoni Beach

Colourful fish, part of the reef scenery

with the addition of a luxury lodge for deep-sea fishermen.

Turn off the main Mombasa Rd about 50km (31 miles) southest of Likoni.

Shimoni

Another small and run-down town with a significant historic pedigree, Shimoni takes its name ('the Place of the Hole') from a massive 15km (9-mile) long cave which was used as a slave pen. It is possible to explore the cave and see the shackles still bolted into the walls. Take a powerful torch and wear sensible shoes.

In the late 19th century, Shimoni was also the first and short-lived headquarters of the Imperial British East Africa Company, under Sir William Mackinnon. Today, it is increasingly popular as the jumping-off point for some of Kenya's best deep-sea fishing grounds and coral reefs. As yet, however, there is little development.

Coral gardens

There are now three conservation areas in the coral gardens off the Shimoni coast; the **Wasini Marine National Park**, in the waters south of Wasini Island, and surrounding three smaller coral islands just off its coast; the 28sq km (11sq mile) **Kisite Marine National Park** and the 11sq km (4sq mile) **Mpunguti National Reserve**, which together form one block a little further out to sea.

Fringed with anemones and decorated by star fish, the reefs here are truly spectacular. Great shoals of shimmering psychedelic fish create an enchanting kaleidoscope of ever-changing colour. The coral here is alive and healthy, as yet largely undamaged by anchors and clumsy flippers.

Wasini Island

A small island (only 17sq km/6½sq miles), Wasini is a delightful place for walking. Only a pillar tomb set with Chinese porcelain remains of the ancient Arab settlement, but the fishing village is a friendly place. Try beachcombing – there are plenty of fragments of pottery and glass as well as marine life in the rock pools.

Shimoni is 100km (62 miles) south of Mombasa. Turn off the main road to the Tanzanian border at Ramisi and Shimoni is 3km (2 miles) further on. At Shimoni, the Pemba Channel Lodge (tel: (0722) 205 020. www.pembachannel.com) and Shimoni Reef Lodge (tel: (041) 471 771/2. www.shimonireeflodge.com) both arrange trips to the National Park. On Wasini Island itself, Mpunguti Lodge and Restaurant (tel: (040) 52288.

www.wasini-lodge.com) and Charlie Claw's (tel: (040) 320 2331. www.wasiniislandkenya.com) do day trips to the reef, often with a memorable seafood lunch. Shimoni Reef Lodge is also pioneering a long-distance marine safari.

Tiwi Beach

The first stretch of the south coast to be developed, Tiwi has now carved itself out a niche as the backpackers' paradise, the only beach near Mombasa to offer a reasonable selection of self-catering and low-budget accommodation. This is one of the widest beaches on the coast. Though usually a pristine coral sand strip, Tiwi Beach can also have a lot of seaweed. The Mwachema River estuary divides Tiwi from Diani Beach and at low tide, it is possible to wade across to the Mwana Mosque.

Mount Kilimanjaro, Africa's highest mountain, at 5,895m (19,341ft)

Turn off the main Mombasa Rd about 20km (12½ miles) south of Likoni. The beach is 3km (2 miles) from the turning. Do not walk along this stretch of road as it is notorious for muggings.

SOUTHERN GAME PARKS
Amboseli National Park

Second in popularity only to the Masai Mara, Amboseli covers 329sq km (127sq miles) on the Tanzanian border. Rarely reaching over 1,000m (3,281ft), most of the land is low and flat, and covered by grassland, with fringes of acacia woodland. The name 'Amboseli' means 'salty dust' in the language of the Maasai. It owes its existence to springs which emerge in the Amboseli swamps at the margins of the Kilimanjaro lavas. During the dry season – the time of the 'salty dust' – these springs are the focus for animals of many species. As you draw near the springs, the concentration of game intensifies. Closer still, buffalo and elephant wallow in the mud, while around them crowd yellow-billed oxpeckers and cattle egrets, picking the ticks off their backs and snapping at insects churned up by their feet.

The western end of the park is occupied by Lake Amboseli, which fluctuates from being a wide, shallow lake, full of birdlife, to a flat and dusty saltpan.

240km (149 miles) southeast of Nairobi. Tel: (045) 225 501. There are several good lodges and campsites. Access by road and air. Open: daily 6am–7pm. Admission charge.

Shimba Hills National Reserve

This small reserve covers 192sq km (74sq miles) of low-lying hills. Much of it is covered by the dense forest which once stretched over the whole coastal area, and many of its giant trees are thought to be over 1,000 years old. There is a high concentration of game here, including Kenya's only herd of the magnificent sable antelope, but the undergrowth is so thick that the animals can be hard to spot. The best way to see them is to stay overnight at Shimba Lodge (*tel: (040) 222 9608. www.aberdaresafarihotels.com*) a tree-hotel built above a waterhole and salt lick.

30km (18½ miles) southwest of Mombasa; the access road is just north of Diani Beach. Open: daily 6am–6pm. Admission charge.

KILIMANJARO

Although actually in Tanzania, Mount Kilimanjaro ('the shining mountain') is one of the great sights of southern Kenya. Dominating the surrounding landscape, its smooth, rounded, ice-capped summit floats in the sky like a giant, cream-topped Christmas pudding. If you wish to see it clearly, get up at dawn when, for an hour or so after sunrise, the sparkling, snow-covered summit may be visible.

At 5,895m (19,341ft), Kilimanjaro is the highest mountain in Africa and also the largest free-standing mountain in the world. In geological terms it is young, a dormant volcano thrown up a million years ago. The fit and determined can climb it with relative ease, although to start an ascent you must go to Arusha in Tanzania; information from the Mountain Club of Kenya (*see p159*).

Taita Hills

When Tsavo National Park was created, the 1,000m (3,281ft) high Taita Hills were being used for agriculture and the boundary looped round them. The sisal plantations are now defunct and much of the area has been converted into a private game sanctuary almost enclosed by, and acting as an extension of, Tsavo. Because of the hills, this is a green, well-watered area, more heavily populated with game than the park itself. The sanctuary's lodges have created their own waterholes and salt licks and lay bait for nocturnal predators. You can go on night drives and guided walks and there are balloon flights (*see pp134–5*) from the Taita Hills Lodge.

Tsavo National Park

Originally designated a national park in 1948, covering a massive 20,812sq km (8,036sq miles) (over 4 per cent of Kenya's total area), Tsavo proved too unwieldy to police and was immediately split into two, Tsavo East and West. The park varies in height from 200m to 2,000m (656–6,562ft),

Mzima Springs, a beautiful oasis in Tsavo West National Park

but the vast majority is made up of dry, flat plains.

There is a wide range of animals and birds here, but Tsavo has traditionally been famous for its elephants. In the 1950s, before the poachers got to work, there were some 40,000 here, including many huge tuskers – enough for the elephants to strip away all the natural heavy woodland, leaving behind the grass and shrubs that are the main vegetation today. By the time the ivory ban was implemented in 1989, there were under 5,000 elephants left. Since then their number has gradually increased. It is presently about 8,000 and increasing. The elephants love bathing in the pervasive red dust and it is said that by moonlight this is the only place in the world to see real pink elephants.

Tsavo East

Because it is so accessible, Tsavo has always been one of the most popular of Kenya's parks, but there are huge areas completely closed to the public, such as the area of Tsavo East north of the Galana River. The southern, accessible section of the park includes the **Kanderi Swamp** and the man-made **Aruba Dam** on the Voi River, both of which have high concentrations of game. Aruba Dam is presently dry, largely due to lack of control of water usage in the Taita Hills. The **Voi Safari Lodge**, near the southern boundary, is set up on a cliff top overlooking a waterhole in what must be one of the most dramatic settings in the country.

Elephant numbers are slowly beginning to recover following the ban on ivory trading

Tsavo West

In the northwestern corner of Tsavo West is the **Shetani Lava Flow**, a massive 50sq km (19sq mile) lava bed. The name means 'devil' in Swahili, and this eerie field of black rock was created some time in the last 500 years by an eruption in the nearby Chyulu Hills, where you can still see the raw cone at the centre of the drama.

Nearby, the **Mzima Springs** form a delightful oasis. The water at Mzima comes from the nearby Chyulu Hills, contrary to the Tsavo River, just to the south, which rises on the slopes of Kilimanjaro. A massive 282,000 litres (62,115 gallons) per minute pump to the surface, of which a small fraction is diverted into a pipeline to form Mombasa's main water supply. The rest joins the Tsavo River, 7km (4 miles) away. Since 1967, visitors have been able to use a submerged viewing tank to observe hippos, crocodiles and barbel underwater.

Tsavo is roughly halfway between Mombasa and Nairobi (around 220km/137 miles to each), and the main road and railway line run right through the park. Due to the security situation, a convoy system is currently operating on the road from Amboseli to the western section of Tsavo. Tsavo East tel: (043) 30049; Tsavo West tel: (045) 22455. Open: daily 6am–6pm. Admission charge. Tsavo East and West have a wide range of accommodation, from camping and simple bandas (huts) to well-appointed lodges such as Kilaguni, Finch Hattons and a brand new lodge at Kitani.

Slaves and spice

The ruined slaving port of Jumba La Mtwana, whose name means 'House of Slaves'

In the 7th century AD, Arab and Persian traders brought their *dhows* to the east African coast to trade, and stayed to marry local women. So was born the Swahili people, their name derived from the Arab word *sahel*, which simply means coast. They are not one group, but an array of different tribes drawn together by a common language.

The Arabs brought with them the new religion of Islam, together with education, an urban lifestyle and sophisticated architecture. They built cities of cool, elaborately decorated houses with indoor plumbing and lush garden courtyards.

By the 14th century, they had entered a golden era, trading with Arabia, India and China for glass, porcelain and fine fabrics. Gold, ivory, tortoiseshell and spices were given in exchange, as well as more mundane products such as grain and dried fish. Above all, however, they were slavers, raiding deep into the hinterland, an occupation that has created a profound and lasting mistrust between the coastal and highland peoples.

Nearly destroyed in a series of savage attacks by the Somali Galla tribe in the 17th century, the Swahili had a second flourish of wealth under Omani rule from the 18th to 19th centuries. This only came to an end when they were forced to stop slaving in 1873. Soon after, they came under British rule, and the British wanted control of the trade routes for themselves.

Today, few of the ancient Swahili families survive and while their *dhows* still trade along the coast, they have been largely superseded by modern ships. Still devoutly Muslim, most of the Swahili people now live in small towns and villages, leading more humble lives as farmers and fishermen.

Mombasa's old slave harbour, now used only by elderly fishing *dhows*

The North

Draw a rough line across the map of Kenya from Kitale in the west to the Tana River delta in the east, via Lake Baringo and Isiolo, and everything above it (over two-thirds of the country's area) is termed the North. It is remote, isolated and forbidding. The roads have grandiose names like the Trans-East African Highway or the Great North Road, but in truth, they are often little more than dirt tracks.

There are some small patches of lush green mountain, but much of the area is desert scrub where only the hardiest trees and bushes cling to a precarious life, their long tap roots sucking up moisture from deep underground reservoirs. There are many riverbeds, but they are all dry, only coming to life during infrequent flash floods when brief heavy rains cannot penetrate the rock-hard earth. The contrast from the bright and fertile green of the Central Highlands could not be greater.

The population density is naturally low and the people need a special resourcefulness to survive in an area of such unreliable rainfall. Drought is the norm, and is interspersed with flash floods that wash away the soil.

It is in the north where the pastoral life of the Turkana and Samburu is most under threat. Repeated droughts in recent decades have resulted in these proud people begging by the roadside, and international food aid was required as recently as 2009.

One success story, however, is the irrigation project on the Wewe River, a tributary of the Kerio, near Marich Pass. Here, using the water flowing from the Cherangani Mountains, seeds of many crops are raised and sold throughout East Africa.

The only stop on the main tourist circuit is the Samburu National Reserve, just north of Isiolo. A few more adventurous people will fly, or make the long drive up to Lake Turkana, and a mere handful now fly in to Marsabit National Park. This is the environment for the traveller truly wanting to experience wild, lonely places, and to add to the normal, very real dangers of desert travel, much of this area has effectively been declared out of bounds due to the occasional armed incursions of Somali bandits.

Maralal

'We arrived in the colourful town of Maralal to discover it wasn't!' is how one disgruntled tourist put it. There is a

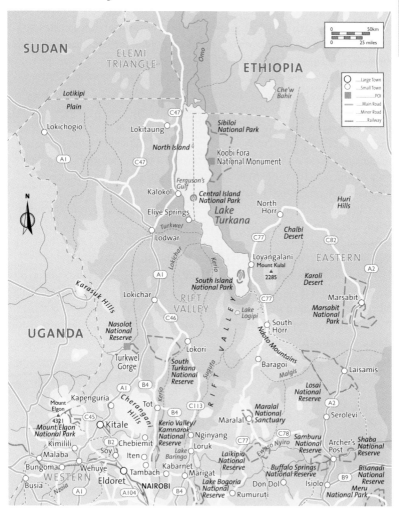

SUDAN

ELEMI TRIANGLE

ETHIOPIA

Omo

Che'w Bahir

Lotikipi Plain

Lokichogio

Lokitaung

C47

North Island

C47

Sibiloi National Park

Koobi Fora National Monument

Ferguson's Gulf

Kalokol

Eliye Springs

Central Island National Park

Lake Turkana

North Horr

Huri Hills

Turkwel

Lodwar

A1

Lokichar

Kerio

South Island National Park

Loyangalani
Mount Kulal
▲
2285

Chalbi Desert

C77

C82

EASTERN

A2

Karoli Desert

Karasuk Hills

Lokichar

RIFT VALLEY

C46

Lake Logipi

South Horr

Marsabit

Marsabit National Park

UGANDA

Nasolot National Reserve

Turkwel Gorge

Lokori

South Turkana National Reserve

Suguta

Ndoto Mountains

Baragoi

Malgis

Laisamis

Losai National Reserve

A2

Mount Elgon

Kapenguria

Tot

Cherangani Hills

A1

B4

Kerio

C113

R I F T   V A L L E Y

Maralal National Sanctuary

Serolevi

4321
Mount Elgon National Park

C45

Kitale

Kerio Valley/ Kamnarok National Reserve

B4

Maralal

C78

Samburu National Reserve

Archer's Post

Shaba National Reserve

Kimilili

Chebiemit

Soy

B2

Nginyang

Loruk

C77

Ewaso Nyiro

Malaba

Iten

Lake Baringo

Laikipia National Reserve

Buffalo Springs National Reserve

Bisanadi National Reserve

Bungoma

Busia

Wehuye

Tambach

Eldoret

A1

WESTERN

Nzoia

Marigat

NAIROBI

Kabarnet

A104

B4

Lake Bogoria National Reserve

Rumuruti

Don Dol

Isiolo

B9

Meru National Park

Legend:
- ○ Large Town
- ○ Small Town
- ■ POI
- Main Road
- Minor Road
- Railway

0 — 50km
0 — 25 miles

N

tendency to hype up the town, mainly because it is the last outpost of any sort of civilisation on the long haul up to Turkana. In fact, it is a pleasant little place set in attractive hills that offer some excellent bush walking. In town, there is a small, lively market and the

lodge has a private game park with a large herd of eland. It has some claims to fame; on the hill above the Maralal is the house in which Jomo Kenyatta spent seven years under house arrest, and the famous explorer Wilfred Thesiger lived in the town until the

1990s. Most of all, for the tourist, it acts as a base for camel trekking, walking and white-water safaris on the Ewaso Nyiro River, about two hours' drive away (*see also pp138–41 for more information on safaris*).

Even if you are not going to Turkana, head north for about 30km (19 miles) to **Moridjo**, where there are two utterly spectacular viewing points as the mountains plunge in an almost sheer drop of some 2,000m (6,562ft) into the **Suguta Valley**, one of the hottest and most inhospitable regions of the planet. In late afternoon, the light is like a Hollywood set for Armageddon.
344km (214 miles) north of Nairobi via Naivasha and Nyaharuru.

Northern Parks and Reserves

By far the most important northern reserve is **Samburu**, together with adjacent **Buffalo Springs** and **Shaba**, all now part of the normal tourist trail. The security threat which existed up to the end of the 1990s has now largely been eliminated.

On the edge of the desert outback, due east of Meru (*see pp68–9*), is a huge cluster of interlinked parks, around the upper reaches of the Tana River. They are **Meru National Park** (*tel: (0164) 20613*), and the **Bisanadi**, **Kora**, **North Kitui** and **Rahole** national reserves. Together they cover 5,281sq km (2,039sq miles) and encompass almost every form of habitat, from Meru's open woodlands to the dense bush of North Kitui and the dry scrub of Bisanadi. Meru is the most famous, the most accessible, and the only one with visitor facilities. This is where the Adamsons did much of their research (*see p59*) and where Joy Adamson was

The giraffe-necked gerenuk is found only in the semi-desert of northern Kenya

Grevy's zebra, with their large ears and pop-art stripes, are found only in the North

murdered. George Adamson later moved his base to Kora, where he too was murdered. The Meru-Kora-Tanu River ecosystem is presently receiving a large injection of aid from Agence Française de Développement, aimed at developing and restoring the tourist infrastructure.

Directly north of Samburu are the impenetrable, volcanic **Losai National Reserve** and the **Marsabit National Park**. Marsabit is a densely forested mountain park containing two beautiful crater lakes. It was traditionally famous for its giant tuskers, among them President Kenyatta's favourite elephant, Ahmed (*see p45*). Poachers slaughtered many of them, but it is still an elephant stronghold, as well as having large herds of greater kudu and many predatory

birds, including lammergeiers. It is possible to fly into the park and there is a lodge as well as camping facilities.

Finally come the tiny **Nasolot** and the **South Turkana** national reserves of completely undeveloped scrubby desert to the north of the Marich Pass on the Kitale–Lodwar road.

THE CAMEL DERBY

At the end of September each year, the Yare Safaris Hostel (4km/2½ miles west of Maralal) plays host to the Maralal International Camel Derby. An increasingly popular day of sheer mayhem, races are open to all who care to rent a camel, from rank amateurs to international racing jockeys.

In 1993, the first truly gruelling endurance race with huge prizes was run across the deserts of northern Kenya in the month leading up to Derby Day. This has become an annual event.

Samburu Lodge, a haven of comfort on the Ewaso Nyiro River

Samburu and environs

Beyond the prairie-like highlands to the north of Mount Kenya, the road falls dramatically by over 1,000m (3,821ft) to the hot, dusty lava plains that mark the start of the northern dry plains. Here, three easily accessible national reserves on the banks of the Ewaso Nyiro River have become popular stops on the tourist trail. Of the three, the most famous is **Samburu** (239sq km/92sq miles), but it shares a boundary along the river with **Buffalo Springs** (131sq km/51sq miles) and the two act, in effect, as one park. Nearby **Shaba** (239sq km/92sq miles) is far less visited.

At an altitude of between 700 and 1,500m (2,297–4,921ft), the landscape is dry and stony, punctuated by small rocky hills, while the vegetation is made up of myriad forms of thorny acacia from small bushes to great yellow-trunked fever trees. The main reason for visiting these parks is to see reticulated giraffe, Grevy's zebra and elephants (*see* Fauna, *pp10–21*). However, there are also large herds of Beisa oryx and Grant's gazelle, and, for the really lucky, the rocky hills provide the perfect habitat for leopards. Samburu is yet another great venue for birds, with over 300 recorded species. *About 30km (19 miles) north of Isiolo. Buffalo Springs and Samburu lead directly off the main road to the left, Shaba is a short distance off the main road to the right. Report in to the police post at Isiolo to check safety before continuing north. All three have lodges and campsites. Open: daily 6am–6pm. Admission charge.*

Turkana

Lake Turkana shines like jade, full of promise but barren. Black volcanic lava stretches, unbroken by a blade of grass, to bare, brown hills until the sight of a living tree is cause for excitement. It is compellingly beautiful and cruel.

The greatest and most northerly of Kenya's Rift Valley lakes, Turkana is 257km (160 miles) long, averages 31km (19 miles) in width and covers an area of 6,750sq km (2,606sq miles), of which 6,400sq km (2,471sq miles) are in Kenya. Fed from the north by the Omo River, which sweeps down off the Ethiopian Highlands, it was, until 2 million years ago, a freshwater lake. Today, Lake Turkana has no outlet, and,

as with all lakes, is gradually silting up. Although technically a soda lake, its alkaline water is only just drinkable.

The first European explorers to visit Turkana, Count Samuel Teleki von Szek and Lieutenant Ludwig von Höhnel, arrived in 1888 and named it after Crown Prince Rudolf of Austria. At first sight, they described it as 'a pearl of great price'. Next day they realised the lake's inhospitable nature, and that even their own lives were at risk. Höhnel wrote: '. . . like some threatening spectre rose up before our minds the full significance of the utterly barren, dreary nature of the lake district. Into what a desert had we been betrayed!'

(*Cont. on p132*)

The North

The dried-up Turkwell Gorge, southern Turkana

The cradle of mankind

Since the 1920s, the story of prehistory in east Africa has been the story of the Leakey family. Louis and Mary Leakey spent a lifetime excavating and studying prehistoric sites along the Rift Valley. At the famous Olduvai Gorge in northern Tanzania, they pushed the date of mankind's origin back about 1.8 million years. In 1967, their son Richard discovered the Koobi Fora fossil site on Lake Turkana (see p129). Here he not only found an almost intact skeleton of a *Homo erectus* boy, about 1.6 million years old, but through other finds, extended the history of mankind back another million years to about 2.9 million years ago.

The Rift Valley offers perfect conditions for the study of human prehistory. The relatively recent volcanic activity covered and preserved many remains, much in the same way as the eruption of Vesuvius froze Pompeii in time. The upward heave of the valley walls has laid these strata open to erosion by wind

The Great Rift Valley was the birthplace of humanity

Stone tools found at several valley sites

and rain. In some cases, the fossils lie on the surface, waiting for archaeologists to recognise them.

The picture emerging today is very different from the straight linear path of evolution that was believed for so long. During the Pliocene era (1–3 million years ago), the first recognisable modern African mammals were evolving. At the same time, it now seems, three different species of proto-humans – gracile australopithecines, *Paranthropus robustus* and *Homo habilis* – lived side by side for over a million years. However, this is a field in which whole theories can rest on a single bone, and the picture is still far from clear. What is evident is that the East

African Rift has provided a wealth of specimens, many far older than those found elsewhere, and has an increasingly solid claim to being the birthplace of humanity. Most recently, Maeve Leakey, wife of Richard Leakey, found the skull of *Kenyanthropus platyops* (flat-faced Kenyan man), a new candidate for man's ancestor.

Probably the most accessible prehistoric site is at Olorgesailie National Park (*see p51*), about 80km (50 miles) south of Nairobi on the Magadi road. It has a small museum and also a campsite.

Lewa is a further prehistoric site. Hand axes from the Acheulean period (800,000–1 million years ago) are found in abundance.

Mount Kulal, overlooking Loyangalani

This area is part of the Sahel, the zone just north of the equator, stretching across Africa, and is always a gamble for the people who live there. In recent decades recurrent drought has brought awful consequences for the people there, in Sudan, Ethiopia and in northern Kenya; many have died from famine. *The easiest way to get to Lake Turkana is by air, but for the adventurous, overland safaris add to the mind-blasting impact of the terrain (see pp138–41).*

Loyangalani

An obscure little settlement, ironically made more interesting by the drought as the normally nomadic Turkana have moved into town. This whole area is part of the 7,000sq km (2,703sq mile) **Mount Kulal Biosphere Reserve**, set up by UNESCO for the study of arid lands. Rising up behind the town to 2,285m (7,497ft), Mount Kulal itself is an oasis of misty montane forest amid the lava flows and craters. It can be climbed by the fit and well equipped.

North of Loyangalani, the El Molo tribe (the smallest in Kenya with under 500 members) fish and hunt crocodiles for food. Their island homes are flimsy, basket-like affairs in which the children and goats live side by side. Off the shore, the 39sq km (15sq mile) **South Island** is the tip of a volcano, completely covered in volcanic ash and home only to the odd wild goat. *On the eastern shore of Lake Turkana, a very long 240km (149 miles) north of Maralal. There are two campsites and one lodge. The El Molo village, 6km (4 miles) north of the town, can be reached by a causeway or canoe. The admission charge includes all photography. Hire a boat in town for the 13km (8-mile) round trip to South Island, but beware of sudden storms.*

Sibiloi National Park

An area of 1,570sq km (606sq miles) around the **Koobi Fora** fossil beds (*see p130*) has been designated a national park to preserve finds for future archaeologists. Discovered accidentally by Dr Richard Leakey in 1967, this desolate spot has become one of the most important areas for prehistoric research in the world.

120km (75 miles) north of Loyangalani. If you are dedicated enough to try to get there, hire a plane or a boat from Ferguson's Gulf, on the western shore of Lake Turkana (access via Kitale and Lodwar).

The reticulated giraffe towers above all in Sibiloi National Park

Getting away from it all

The whole point of a holiday in Kenya is to get away from it all. Many of the listings in the Destination Guide take you far out into the bush. Getting away from it all here really means getting away from other tourists, leaving behind the trappings of sophistication.

The vast majority of the tourists on the coast stay within the stretch from Malindi to Diani Beach. Head north to Lamu or south to Funzi and Shimoni, and you are away from the crowd. Inland, there is a well-worn tourist path to the Masai Mara, Samburu, the Rift Valley lakes, Amboseli and Tsavo. In any of the other game parks, you will leave the herd behind. Even within these most popular parks, it is easy to shrug off the flock of minibuses if you venture into the remoter sections, away from the lodges and airstrips. There are virtually no tourists at all in western Kenya beyond the Mara, so head over to Lake Victoria or up to Mount Elgon. North of Baringo, the number of other tourists dwindles to a mere trickle, while beyond Maralal, on the road to Lake Turkana, you will feel as if you have stepped off the edge of the known world.

Ballooning

It is so expensive that many people regard a balloon trip as a once in a lifetime treat. The problem with this is that once in the air, you never want to come down and once reluctantly back on the ground, all you can dream of is how to afford another ride.

Up in pitch darkness, blinking and shivering, you arrive at the launch site just as the balloon puffs out, its gaudy envelope and the streak of orange flame the only spot of brilliance in the monochrome of early dawn. As you are instructed on how to brace yourself for landing and take-off, it billows high above the trees – so much larger than expected. You climb in, the rim of the basket is reassuringly high and turn to look at the great jets of flame from the burners, while the ground floats gently away from you. You are drifting high above the trees, but there is no sensation of movement and no sense of panic at being suspended in a basket so far up above the earth.

The sun turns sky and grass alike to gold; below, a herd of nervous wildebeest skitter away from the balloon's shadow. The sharp-eyed pilot points out a cheetah slinking through the grass, a trail of dust across the plains marks the progress of the chase vehicles.

The game viewing is good, but it becomes almost irrelevant in the whole glorious experience. As the pilot starts, all too soon, to search for a suitable landing place, away from water and free of lions, you find yourself willing him to go on forever. Your heart crashes back to earth with a bump bigger than that of the basket. All that saves you from dejection

is the champagne breakfast laid out behind the rise, a gourmet picnic fit for a king.

Balloon trips operate in the Masai Mara, Taita Hills, near Tsavo, the Chyulus and at Soysambo (Lake Elementeita). Most safari companies include them as an optional extra. Alternatively, contact:

Adventures Aloft, Siana Springs. *Tel: (020) 600 5328. www.madahotels.com*
Transworld Safaris. *Tel: (020) 445 1620. www.transworldsafaris.com*

Balloon safaris can offer amazing views

Boating

One of the best ways of getting away is to take to the water, whether on a raft over Class V rapids, on a seagoing yacht with the prospect of wrestling marlin, or a leisurely meander through the mangrove swamps on a *dhow* under sail.

Tana Delta camp

This is a 15-minute boat trip from the landing stage on the Tana River and combines boating with serious 'get-away-from-it-all' safaris.
Tana Delta Ltd, PO Box 24988, Nairobi. Tel/fax: (020) 882 826/(020) 882 939. www.tanadelta.org

Deep-sea fishing

See p161.

Dhows

There are few sights more elegant than a *dhow* in full sail, and nothing more peaceful than sitting on board, trailing a hand through the spray as the wind catches the great triangular sail and the bow slices through a gentle sea. There are some very upmarket *dhow* trips in Mombasa (*see p154*) which are a totally different and very worthwhile experience. For the truly offbeat adventure, however, head north to Lamu, and take a day trip to nearby islands or venture further afield and sleep under the stars (*see pp94–5 & pp98–9*). True addicts, with time to spare, can hire a *dhow* for a longer, coast-hugging journey down to

Mombasa or even as far as Zanzibar. Sail by day, camp at night around a bonfire, and live on what you can catch over the side.

Lake Victoria

Gone, sadly, are the days when the lake steamer linked Kenya and Tanzania with Uganda. Now the elderly ferry does a slow shuffle along the lake shore between Kisumu, Kendu Bay and Homa Bay. There are three classes, but do remember that this is local transport, rarely touched by tourists, so don't expect too much, even of first class. You should be able to buy drinks and sandwiches on board, but take your own supplies just in case.

The journey takes five hours each way and you will have to arrange for return transport, unless you wish to trust to the local bus or *matatus*.

Other local ferries, resembling overgrown canoes, travel between the inhabited islands and you can hire a boat from the local fishermen to take you out to one of the island game parks or just for a ride.
Tickets for the ferry are available from the jetty offices, just behind the Railway Station in Kisumu and next to the hotel in Homa Bay.

WHITE-WATER RAFTING

Kenya has three rivers suitable for rafting – the Tana, the Athi and the Ewaso Nyiro. Most levels of competence can be found, from gentle eddying backwaters to Class V white water to equal the toughest in the world. **Savage Wilderness Safaris** organise tailor-made rafting trips, from gentle one-day excursions to two-week surfeits, though most people find three to four days plenty. You can decide the level of comfort you require (and are willing to pay for), from a bivouac and bonfire to the full works with showers, four-course meals and wine.

Savage Wilderness Safaris, PO Box 1000, Sarit Centre, Nairobi. Tel: (020) 712 1590. www.whitewaterkenya.com

A *dhow* under sail off the coast of Mombasa

Getting away from it all

ON SAFARI
The essence of a holiday in Kenya

Safari is Swahili for 'journey', but the word has grown to have a much more focused meaning in the mind of the traveller. Safari conjures up big game, the African night, the vast plains; maybe camping, or a luxurious lodge, deep in the bush. To go 'on safari' is the quintessential African holiday and is unlike any other.

Planning your safari – some decisions

The first thing to decide is what you wish to experience. Do you want guaranteed masses of animals, such as the river crossings in the Masai Mara or the daily elephant trek to the Amboseli swamps? Or something quieter and more remote, in a less popular area? In one you will share your safari with other people; in the other you can be almost alone in the wilderness.

Lodge or camp

Lodges are really 4-star hotels in the bush. On your game drive you are in the bush, but at the lodge you will enjoy all the convenience of a hotel.

Camps range from utter luxury in a permanent location, with facilities similar to a high-class lodge, to a small, perhaps mobile camp, erected just for you and a few others (an experience similar to that enjoyed by Meryl Streep and Robert Redford in *Out of Africa*).

Fly or drive

Driving is more tiring and often very dusty, but it puts you in close contact with the people, the animals and the land. Flying is quick and gives you more time for your actual 'safari'. It may also give you superb views of Mount Kenya, Kilimanjaro and the Rift Valley. But it keeps you at arm's length from the real Africa.

There are about 15 air charter companies in Kenya. Check with your safari company or Let's Go Travel (*see* *pp140–41*).

How much to spend?

There is an enormous range of possibilities, from one hundred dollars a day to a few thousand.

KENYA WILDLIFE SERVICE NATIONAL PARK CONTACTS

Aberdares	*Tel: (061) 550 24121*
Amboseli	*Tel: (045) 22251*
Baringo	*Tel: (053) 22047*
Hell's Gate	*Tel: (050) 50407*
Lamu	*Tel: (042) 33080*
Malindi Marine	*Tel: (042) 20845*
Marsabit	*Tel: (069) 2028*
Meru	*Tel: (064) 20613*
Mombasa Marine	*Tel: (041) 231 2744*
Mount Elgon	*Tel: (054) 310456*
Mount Kenya	*Tel: (061) 55645*
Mount Longonot	*Tel: (050) 50255*
Nairobi	*Tel: (020) 602121*
Nakuru	*Tel: (051) 41078*
Saiwa Swamp	*Tel: (054) 55022*
Shimba Hill	*Tel: (040) 4159*
Tsavo East	*Tel: (043) 30049*
Tsavo West	*Tel: (056) 22120*

Kenya Wildlife Service HQ
www.kws.org
kws@kws.org

The architecture of lodges often has a strong tribal influence

In general, the more exclusive the safari is (though not necessarily the more comfortable), the more expensive it will be.

If you have time, shop around, especially at the top end of the range. Ask how big the tents are, how well furnished and equipped they are, the choice of food and how many people share each vehicle.

Safari organisers

Most holiday companies in the high streets of the UK, Europe and North America will include safari holidays to Kenya. These will normally be packages, usually to the more popular locations, though not exclusively. They may include a combination of 'beach and bush'.

In Nairobi there are many companies which will access the entire range of

MAPS AND BOOKS

Your safari will be much enhanced if you know where you are and if you can identify what you see.

Far and away the best maps are those coming on to the market from Jacana, with new surveys and cartography by award-winning Harvey Maps. Present titles are *Mara Triangle*, *Masai Mara* and *Amboseli*. Other available maps are generally too inaccurate for navigation.

For birds, try the new *Field Guide to the Birds of East Africa* by Stevenson and Fanshawe.

For animals, Jonathan Kingdom's *Kingdom Pocket Guide to African Mammals* is more than adequate.

safari options and can arrange absolutely everything for you, according to your wishes. The best of these is undoubtedly **Let's Go Travel**, with various locations in Nairobi.

It can be dusty close to stampeding animals

Getting away from it all

A dismembered tree stops a young elephant in his tracks

PO Box 60342-00200 Nairobi.
Head Office 1st Floor, ABC Place,
Waiyaki Way, Westlands, Nairobi.
Tel: (020) 444 7151/444 1030.
Fax: (020) 444 7270/444 1690.
www.uniglobeletstravel.com
Other companies manage the bookings
for a number of lodges or camps.
They will include a range of prices,
but generally are at the top end of
the market.

Try **Abercrombie and Kent**, **Bush and
Beyond** or **Cheli Peacock**. Abercrombie
and Kent offer bespoke safaris.
www.abercrombiekent.com
Bush and Beyond manage about
12 locations.
Tel: (020) 600 457/605 108.
www.bush-and-beyond.com
Cheli Peacock manage 14 high-
class camps.
www.chelipeacock.com

The 'Lunatic Line'

When the Imperial British East Africa Company decided to build a railway line inland from their fledgling colony at Mombasa, no one knew quite what was at the other end. Only a handful of Europeans had ever explored the area and there was absolutely no development to create a market for either freight or passenger traffic. At a projected cost of £3.5 million, it was one of the most unlikely gambles in colonial history. Henry Labouchère's satirical poem (*opposite*) was only one of a frenzy of objections.

Construction on the 935km (581-mile), metre-gauge track began in 1896. From the start, it proved eventful. All building materials travelled to Kenya via Bombay; a new harbour was built at Kilindini to handle the volume of cargo. A total of 33,000 Indians were imported through the years as construction workers.

The line wends its way west through the Kikuyu Highlands

The Lunatic Line needed massive locomotives

The line ran through swamp, forest and desert, crossed the Rift Valley and climbed to over 2,743m (9,000ft). There were horrendous problems with theft by local tribespeople, who took the copper wire for jewellery and the rails for weapons. Disease stalked the camps and 28 Indian workers, together with, perhaps, 60 native Africans fell prey to man-eating lions, which became famous as the 'man-eaters of Tsavo' before the culprits were eventually shot, stuffed and put on display in a Chicago museum. Even today, Tsavo lions are believed to be more *kali* or fierce than those in other areas of Kenya.

In 1899, Nairobi was founded as a railhead. By the time the line reached Kisumu on the shores of Lake Victoria, in 1901, settlers had followed it inland to what proved to be some of the world's most fertile farmlands. The railway to nowhere had created a colony.

'What it will cost no words can express;
What is its object no brain can suppose;
Where it will start from no one can guess;
Where it is going to nobody knows.
What is the use of it none can conjecture;
What it will carry there's none can define;
And in spite of George Curzon's
    superior lecture
It clearly is naught but a lunatic line.'

TRACKS ACROSS AFRICA

Winston Churchill, who got to sit on a garden seat on the cowcatcher in 1908, described the East African Railway as the most romantic in the world. Its route from Mombasa, inland across the great Tsavo plains, through Nairobi and the Central Highlands, across the Rift Valley and the great tea plantations, to Lake Victoria is staggeringly beautiful. All the regular trains are overnight, however, giving you only tantalising glimpses of the landscape.

Nevertheless, the train is wonderful – old-fashioned and thoroughly atmospheric. First class has two-berth cabins and second has four. Both have fans, private washbasins and plentiful, hygienic toilets. Third class offers uncomfortable seats only. For first and second class, you must book ahead and specify whether you want bedding, dinner and/or breakfast. Meals are flavourless, though worthwhile for the ambience. Served on spotless linen, using china and cutlery left over from the colonial period, the four-course dinner menu seems not to have changed since Mrs Beeton was alive.

In November 2006, a consortium led by Sheltam from South Africa, plus a number of East African investors, agreed to a 25-year concession to run the railway in both Kenya and Uganda. The company will be known as The Rift Valley Railway. Their first job was to re-equip the workshops in Nairobi and then to begin the massive maintenance programme required after years of neglect. In the first few years, the entire fabric of the track will be replaced and a railway fit for the 21st century will gradually emerge.

Bookings via any Kenyan travel agent, many safari companies, or from station booking offices. Nairobi Station, Station Rd, is 1.5km (1 mile) from the city centre; Mombasa Station, Haile Selassie Ave, is a few hundred metres from Moi Ave; Kisumu Station, New Station Rd, stands between the lake shore and town centre.

For up-to-date details of train times consult the Thomas Cook Overseas Timetable, *published bi-monthly, available to buy online at www.thomascookpublishing.com or from Thomas Cook branches in the UK (tel: 01733 416477).*

All aboard the 'Lunatic Line' for the 935km (581-mile) journey from Mombasa to Kisumu, Lake Victoria

Mombasa Station, the start of the line

Shopping

Kenya has almost more souvenir sellers per capita than any other country in the world. There are upmarket shops, street stalls, market stands, wayside curio shops, wandering touts and tribal women with a few trinkets. Every tour guide has deals going with certain shops; every time you walk down the street, or even stop for a drink, a group will miraculously gather.

They are all superb salesmen, pitch an amazing hard-luck story (sadly, often all too true), and haggle until you are ready to drop. What is more, they travel in packs, and as soon as you have made a deal with one, the next steps in. It is often extremely difficult not to buy, and by the time you have 25 unwanted copper bracelets, 10 soapstone rhinos and an alarmingly vicious Maasai spear, you could seriously be questioning your sanity.

The initial price is usually set according to what they think you are willing to spend. Prices start higher on the coast, while an American accent is a real drawback. Luckily, if you bargain hard enough, prices for the often rather poor quality souvenirs at street level can be extremely low. You go away pleased with your haggling skills, while the vendor beams with delight at getting double what it was actually worth.

Prices for real quality are markedly higher, so it is best to stick to the upmarket, fixed price shops. If the price is not displayed, ask for a receipt to avoid opportunistic money-making by the staff.

WHAT TO BUY
Basketware
There are many possibilities, from laundry baskets to brightly coloured trays and placemats. Look out in particular for the sisal *kiondos*, which make excellent handbags. The baskets are used by the Kenyans themselves, so are usually of excellent quality and very hard wearing.

Fabrics
Unless you want to go all out and buy yourself a safari outfit, complete with solar topee, have a good look at the brilliant range of T-shirts. Alternatively, you can buy a *kanga*, the sarong-style cloths worn by local women, with bright designs and often acerbic Swahili proverbs printed on to the hem, or *kikois*, lengths of thicker,

often stripy cloth, traditionally worn by coastal fishermen. There is also a wide range of batiks and wax paintings, many of them of extremely good quality.

Makonde statues

Usually depicting people, these glossy woodcarvings are an imported tradition from Tanzania. Theoretically made of ebony, most are fakes, using lighter woods and boot polish. You can feel the difference by weight (ebony is extremely dense and heavy). It is illegal to carve Kenyan (but not imported) ebony, and ecologically unsound to support the trade. Many sculptures are very crudely carved, so shop around.

A wide range of basketware is available

Stone

Ubiquitous pink and white Kisii soapstone from Western Kenya (*see p91*), comes in every possible incarnation from hippos to ashtrays and chess sets. There are also many beautiful malachite products, from chess sets to bowls, beads and bracelets, at very affordable prices.

Tribal beads

Alongside the array of traditional gourds and calabashes and purely touristy spears and shields is an array of wonderfully bright and intricate beadwork, from earrings to spectacular Maasai wedding necklaces. Easily carried, these make excellent souvenirs, but the workmanship is sometimes shoddy, and because of the amount of detail, they can be surprisingly expensive.

Woodcarvings

Perfect cheap-and-cheerful souvenirs which come in every shape and form, from multitudinous small animals to napkin rings and salad servers and simple, elegant hardwood bowls.

WHERE TO SHOP

Shopping hours are normally from Monday to Saturday, 8.30am to 5.30pm. Some shops close for lunch between 1pm and 2pm; longer at the coast.

Nairobi

Nairobi has many souvenir shops, including galleries selling African artwork, ranging from the 'cheap tourist' to the superb. For good quality, try the malls in the New Stanley and Hilton hotels and Standard Street. In most areas of the city and on arterial roads you will find souvenir shops. For cheaper, reasonable-quality goods, the best place is City Market on Muindi Mbingu Street. For real bargains, try the street stalls along Tom Mboya Street and River Road (not safe on your own), or Kariokor Market, on Racecourse Road. The latter is more like a real market, with thriving local trade as well. The best fabrics and clothes are found in Muindi Mbingu and Biashara streets.

African Heritage Centre

Large store, wide range.
Banda St and Libra House, Mombasa Rd.

Banana Box

Stylish, but expensive.
Sarit Centre, Westlands.

A beach seller at Nyali

Blue Rhino

Famous for their iconic historical maps.

ABC Plaza, Waiyaki Way, Westlands.

Kazuri Beads

Famous range of beads and crockery. Big employer of women, worth supporting.

Mbagathi Ridge, Karen; Junction Shopping Centre and Village Market.

Kitengela Glass

Lovely products in unique designs.

Adams Arcade, Junction Shopping Centre and Village Market.

Marco Polo

Karen; Junction Shopping Centre.

Masai Market

Hundreds of traders. Fridays.

Village Market, Gigiri.

Sandstorm Africa

Lenana Forest Centre.

Spinners' Web

Viking House, Waiyaki Way, Westlands.

Utamaduni

Co-operative with wide range of crafts. Nice café.

Bogani Road East, Langata.

Mombasa

The whole of Moi Avenue is lined with souvenir shops and galleries, while large sections of Moi Avenue and Nyerere Street have grown a second skin of small stalls. The best fabrics are to be found in Biashara Street. In the old town, particularly on Mbarak Hinawy Road, many of the fine old houses have now joined the souvenir trade. You stand a fighting chance of finding something a little different here, with ornate Lamu chests, Ethiopian silver and Arabic coffee sets, along with carvings and bags.

Bombolulu

A rehabilitation centre for the blind and handicapped who make jewellery, hand-printed cotton clothes and leather goods. The workshop tours and factory shop have become a major tourist attraction in their own right.

Malindi Rd, 3km (2 miles) north of Mombasa town. Tel: (041) 471 704. Open: Mon–Fri 7.30am–12.30pm & 2–5pm. Shop open: Mon–Sat 8am–5pm.

Labeka

A real notch above the other shops along Moi Avenue, with beautiful *makonde* carvings as well as antiques, including silver and amber jewellery.

Moi Ave. Tel: (020) 312 232.

Nanyuki

There is a great gathering of souvenir stalls around the equator sign, just south of town, while the Mount Kenya Safari Club houses some extremely upmarket boutiques and galleries (*see p69*).

The Spinners' and Weavers' Co-operative

Founded in 1977, to employ local women who spin, weave, dye, knit and sell a variety of products from rugs to jumpers and gossamer-light shawls.

In the grounds of the Presbyterian Church, Nyeri Rd.

Markets

Markets are everywhere, but are not much frequented by most visitors, especially those on package tours. In the large towns, there are permanent covered markets, with set stalls under barn-like roofs. But where you have

A fruit and vegetable stall at Lamu central market

Tribal shields for sale

more than three houses and a shop, a market will spring up once a week and people will trek in, on foot, by bus, *matatu*, or in battered trucks, from far and wide.

The market square is outlined by a row of dusty shops, brightened by blue and scarlet Bata and Coca-Cola signs. In their gloomy depths, shelves groan under an extraordinary array of biscuits and car parts, text books and ageing tins of jam, while the young men cluster in the doorways, drinking warm sodas. The butcher's shop, as dingy as the rest, is marked by a gaily painted cartoon pig. Under a shady tree, a rusty wheel proclaims the territory of the puncture repair man. Nearby, an itinerant barber has set up shop with

little more than a chair, a bowl of water and a pair of scissors. An old woman crouches behind a smoking brazier, turning her roasting cobs of corn.

Anyone with something to sell just sets up shop, laying a cloth out on the ground to mark their space. On it, they heap mounds of clothes or piles of potatoes. One woman has arrived with two bucket-loads of oranges, another with a goat, a third is doing a roaring trade in recycled maize meal sacks and sandals made from car tyres. And always, somewhere in the general maelstrom, some hopeful person has laid out some beads and bangles, baskets or wooden animals and squats beside them waiting for a tourist to arrive.

Entertainment

There is a wide range of entertainment on offer in Nairobi, a reasonable array in Mombasa and Nyali, a small amount in Malindi and virtually nothing elsewhere. Except in Nairobi, the local social life revolves almost exclusively around the bars. It is impossible to leave your lodge in the game parks and often difficult to get out of the more isolated beach resorts, so these hotels do try to arrange entertainment each evening, from occasional discos and barbecues to videos, lectures and the ubiquitous Maasai dancers.

If you are looking to rave around the clock, stay in Nairobi. To find out what's on, read the entertainment listings in *The Nation* daily newspaper.

CASINOS
Nairobi
Casino de Paradise
Safari Park Hotel, Thika Rd. Tel: (020) 363 3000. www.safaripark-hotel.com. Open: Mon–Fri noon–3am, Sat–Sun & holidays noon–4am.

Celebrities Casino
Esso Plaza. Tel: (020) 766 0540.

Florida Casino
Uhuru Highway & University Way. Tel: (020) 221 4139.

The International Casino
Nairobi's oldest casino, popular with tourists.
Westlands Rd, Museum Hill. Tel: (220) 374 2600.

Mayfair Casino Nairobi
Next to Holiday Inn, Parklands Rd. Tel: (220) 374 3300. Open: Sun–Thur noon–3am; Fri, Sat & holidays noon–4am.

RKL Casino
Inter-Continental Hotel, City Hall Way & Uhuru Highway. Tel: (020) 221 2892. Open: Sun–Thur noon–3am; Fri, Sat & holidays noon–4am.

Mombasa
Golden Key Casino
Stylish and chic with a great view from the terrace.
Rooftop of Tamarind Restaurant, Nyali. Tel: (041) 471 071. www.tamarind.co.ke. Open: daily 3pm–5am.

New Florida Club and Casino
On the waterfront, very popular with tourists and locals.
Mama Ngina Dr, Mombasa. Tel: (041) 231 3127. Open: daily 24 hours.

Malindi
Casino Malindi
Italian-owned, air-conditioned, busy during the tourist season.
Lamu Rd. Tel: (042) 30878. Open: daily 9am–5pm.

CINEMAS

As ever, the only real choice is in Nairobi, which has several good cinemas and numerous fleapits. Prices in them all are a fraction of those in the West. If you have a car, try an evening at one of the two drive-ins; they are really good fun for weather-bound Europeans who have only ever seen them in the movies!

Most of the top Hollywood films make it into the main cinemas, along with an inexhaustible supply of Hindi movies. You may not understand these, but if you have never seen one, choose the one with the most lurid poster and grab the opportunity – they are a mind-blowing experience.

For independent and 'foreign' films, you will need to go to the more select cultural centres, listed below.

Nairobi

Details of films, times, etc are posted daily in all the newspapers.

Fox Cineplex
Modern facilities, Western films.
Sarit Centre, 2nd Floor, Westlands.
Tel: (020) 227 959.

Fox Drive-in Cinema
Local and Western films.
Thika Rd. Tel: (020) 802 293.

Kenya Cinema
Mainly Western films.
Moi Ave. Tel: (020) 227 822.

Nairobi Cinema
Mainly local, some Western films.
Uchumi House, Aga Khan Walk.
Tel: (020) 241 614.

Nu Metro Cinemas
Modern multiplex, latest Western films.
Village Market; Prestige Plaza; The Junction. Tel: (020) 522 128.

Mombasa

Kenya Cinema
Western and Bollywood films.
Moi Ave.

Lotus Cinema
Western and Bollywood films.
Makadara Rd.

Nyali Cinemax
Ultra-modern, air-conditioned. Latest Western and Bollywood films.
Main Nyali Rd. Tel: (041) 470 000.
www.nyalicinemax.com

CULTURAL CENTRES

The various national cultural centres organise a range of activities from film shows to lectures and exhibitions. They are popular with residents and a good place to meet expatriates.

Nairobi

Alliance Française
Loita St. Tel: (020) 340 054.
www.ambafrance-ke.org

American Cultural Centre
National Bank Building, Harambee Ave.
Tel: (020) 337 877.
http://nairobi.usembassy.gov

British Council
Upper Hill Rd, Nairobi Hill.
Tel: (020) 283 6000.
www.britishcouncil.org/kenya

French Cultural Centre
Loita St. Tel: (020) 222 4640.

Entertainment

German Goethe Institute
Maendeleo House, corner Monrovia St
and Loita St. Tel: (020) 222 4640.
www.goethe.de/nairobi

Italian Cultural Institute
Woodvale Grove, off Waiyaki Way.
Tel: (020) 445 1226.
www.iicnairobi.esteri.it

Japan Information Centre
Kumbu Drive. Tel: (020) 566 262.
www.ke.emb-japan.go.jp/jicc.htm

Mombasa

Alliance Française
Freed Building, Moi Ave.
Tel: (041) 340 079.

British Council
Moi Ave. Tel: (041) 222 3076.
www.britishcouncil.org/kenya

DHOW TRIPS

Several companies operate tours in *dhows* around Mombasa Island. All are priced in hard currency and are fairly expensive, but are still worthwhile. The operators will collect you from and deliver you back to your hotel.

Jahazi Marine

Two trips per day, one at midday, and one to Mombasa by night. Payment to be made in US dollars. It is possible to arrange an evening cruise followed by dinner at Fort Jesus.
Tel: (041) 548 5001.
www.severin-kenya.com

Tamarind Dhows

Two trips daily: at lunchtime and at night. The evening cruise is an absolute must, a superbly romantic night under the stars in an elegantly carved *dhow*, overlooking the floodlit waterfront of Mombasa Old Town.
Tel: (041) 474 4600.
www.tamarinddhow.com

MUSIC AND DANCING
Nairobi

Nairobi has a wide range of discos and clubs, from the very sedate to the raucous. Be aware of the risk of pickpockets. Also, at most places men will be pestered by prostitutes, many of whom will be carriers of HIV/AIDS.

Cats Club

Venue for all types of music.
Safari Park Hotel. Tel: (020) 363 300/
356 2222. Open: Mon–Sat.

Florida 2000 and New Florida

Both very trendy and highly popular, especially at weekends.
On Koinange St and Moi Ave,
respectively. Florida 2000,
tel: (020) 221 5014.
New Florida, tel: (020) 222 9036.
www.floridaclubskenya.com

The Green House

Outside bar and restaurant. Local food. Venue for some of Kenya's best bands.
Nyangumi Rd, Hurlingham.
Tel: (075) 543 095.

Ngong Hills Hotel

Nyama choma (roasted meat). Wide range of music, dancing and shows. Very child-friendly at weekends.
Ngong Rd. Tel: (025) 67137.

Pavement Club

Trendy, popular with Nairobi 'in' crowd. Food and music.

Westview Centre, Westlands.
Tel: (020) 444 1711.

Simba Saloon
Popular with Nairobi crowd and young
expats. Plenty of room for dancing.
Hosts international bands.
Part of Carnivore restaurant.
Off Langata Rd. Tel: (020) 501 709.

Mombasa
Casablanca Club
Several bars and discos. Very popular.
Mnazi Moja Rd.

New Florida Club
Very large. Multiple bars and dance
areas. Very popular. Live music.
Mama Ngina Rd. Tel: (041) 313 127.

Toy 2 Disco
Noisy mixture of African music.
Off Nkrumah Rd. Tel: (041) 313 931.

Malindi
Fermento Bar
Large disco. Sometimes live music.
Galana Centre. Tel: (042) 31780.

Stardust
A very popular disco venue for both
tourists and locals.
Lamu Rd, opposite Galana Shopping
Centre. Tel: (042) 20388.

Elsewhere in the country, the only
dancing on offer will be in the local
bars or at the occasional dinner-dance
thrown by a local society.

THEATRE
There are three theatres in Nairobi and
one in Mombasa, all churning out
amateur productions of perennial
favourites from all over the world.

Braeburn Theatre
Litanga Rd, Nairobi. Tel: (020) 567 901.
Kenya National Theatre *Harry Thuku*
Rd, Nairobi. Tel: (020) 313 171.
Phoenix Players *Parliament Rd,*
Nairobi. Tel: (020) 222 5506.
www.phoenixplayers.net

TRIBAL DANCING
Most hotels and lodges will feature
tribal dancing displays at some time
as part of their evening entertainment.
In Maasai areas, which in practice will
include the majority of national parks
and reserves, this will mean some form
of Maasai dancing.

Other African tribes tend to dance to
the drum beat. But the Maasai dance to a
distinctive, rhythmic chanting by a group
of young warriors or *morani*, with high-
pitched interjections by Maasai girls.
Often, tourists are invited to join in.

The Bomas of Kenya
Daily demonstrations of traditional
African dance – noisy, colourful and
great fun. All the dances are performed
by a professional troupe and there is an
accompanying programme which gives
some background.
Forest Edge Rd, Langata.
10km (6 miles) southeast of Nairobi,
off the Langata Rd.
Tel: (020) 891 801/890 793.
www.bomasofkenya.co.ke. Mon–Fri
2.30pm, Sat & Sun 3.30pm, & some
evenings. Admission charge.

Children

Apart from a few places such as Naivasha, all the commercial attractions for children are concentrated in Nairobi and Mombasa, the two cities with a growing middle class and a large expatriate community. Eighty per cent of Kenyan children live in the countryside, and their poverty makes their playthings very simple and 'homespun'.

On the other hand, the whole country is a giant playground, with an excellent climate, wide open spaces to run around in and endless fascinating creatures to look at. There are chances to ride horses and camels, swim, tickle giant tortoises and hold a python. The Africans love small children and will happily include them in any activity.

Supplies
You can buy all the basics, from steriliser to nappies and baby foods in most towns. What you won't find is choice, recognisable labels and instant, throwaway options, so take a large supply of disposable nappies and baby food. Hats, sunblock, sandals and travel sickness pills are essentials.

Babysitting
The chief problem is keeping your children safe. They will be enthralled by their surroundings without any concept of the unfamiliar dangers, and you must ensure that they don't eat peculiar insects or drink stream water given to them by a kindly local mum. Most resort hotels have babysitting facilities, available during the day and in the evening. Many resorts have good play facilities, both indoor and out, and in most hotels an early children's dinner is the norm.

At the coast
Most of the organised attractions, such as crocodile farms and snake parks, are to be found in the Nyali area, north of Mombasa (*see pp111–13*). The resort hotels all have swimming pools and there is easy access to the beach. Older children will love a chance to go snorkelling on the coral reef. Many resorts now have windsurfing, kite-surfing, kayaking and a host of other water-related activities.

On safari
Taking small infants on safari is probably foolhardy. The very long hours of driving over dusty roads in the company of strange adults would be

hell for parents and children alike.

To cut down on the driving, stick to one game park. If you have the money, fly in, stay at a lodge or tented camp with a swimming pool and book game-viewing trips through the hotel. An alternative would be to look at the custom-made private safaris. If there are several of you, it need not be astronomically expensive and you effectively have a private holiday with a staff to help with the practicalities.

Other activities for children in Nairobi include:

Animal Orphanage

Opened in 1964, this organisation cares for orphaned and sick animals from all over Kenya. Animals are released into the wild whenever possible, otherwise they are housed at the Safari Walk. There is a Wildlife Conservation Education Centre with videos and guided tours. Feeding time is at 2.30pm. *Main Gate of the Nairobi National Park, Langata Rd. Tel: (020) 600 800. www.kws.org. Open: daily.*

Butterfly Centre

This large centre offers visitors an in-depth look at the lives of butterflies, with the aim of conserving African butterflies in particular. *Dagoretti Rd, Karen.*

David Sheldrick Wildlife Trust

A wonderful place to visit and support, the Trust is dedicated to the protection and conservation of Africa's wildlife. Elephant feeding time is 11am–noon. *Mbagathi Rd, Mbagathi Gate, Nairobi*

National Park. Tel: (020) 891 996. www.sheldrickwildlifetrust.org

Giraffe Centre

Get up close and personal to these friendly and elegant mammals via a raised platform. *Langata Rd. Tel: (020) 890 952. www. giraffecenter.org. Open: daily 9am–5.30pm.*

Mamba Village

A 12ha (30-acre) park with crocodiles, ostriches, camel rides, boat rides and several places to eat. *Langata Rd. Tel: (020) 891 765. www.nairobimambavillage.com*

Nairobi Safari Walk

Opened as an education centre for local schools, this is a nice walk through a 18ha (44-acre) forest, wetland and savannah park. On-site restaurant. *Main Gate of the Nairobi National Park. Tel: (020) 600 800. www.kws.org*

Sarit Centre

Large shopping centre with a food court, cinema and games hall. *Parklands Rd. Tel: (020) 374 7408. www.saritcentre.com*

Splash Waterworld

Waterslides, swimming pools and an on-site restaurant. *Langata Rd, next to Carnivore restaurant. Tel: (020) 603 777. Open: Mon–Fri 10am–5.30pm, Sat, Sun & holidays 10am–6pm.*

Village Market

Upmarket shopping centre with a bowling alley, cinema and playground. *Limuru Rd. Tel: (020) 712 2488. www.villagemarket-kenya.com*

Sport and leisure

In sport, Kenya is famous for the medals won by its world-beating distance runners and for the Safari Rally. At grass-roots level, football is favourite and many Kenyans are keen supporters of English Premier League clubs. Other popular sports are a relic of colonial days, with several strong rugby clubs in Nairobi. Kenya is also emerging as a cricketing nation and there are over 40 golf courses in the country.

The Asian community keeps up a tradition of cricket and hockey, and some of the wealthier Africans have taken up golf, racing and polo, but on the whole, the more expensive sports have remained the province of Europeans and tourists. Kenya has two large sports venues, both in Nairobi and seriously underused – the Nyayo Stadium on Uhuru Highway and the vast Moi International Stadium on Thika Road, built by the Chinese for the 1987 Pan-Africa Games and capable of holding 60,000 people.

To find out what is on in the way of spectator sports, read *The Nation* sports diary on Saturdays. For participatory sports, see below, or ask at your hotel reception desk.

Aerial sports

Although many Kenyans use small planes, relatively few indulge in other aerial sports. Ballooning is one of the great – and expensive – treats on offer (*see pp134–5*). There is a small gliding club at Mweiga, in the Central Highlands, whose members will take up visitors on an ad hoc basis. Meanwhile, the great cliffs and thermals of the Rift Valley are attracting world-class hang-gliders, starry-eyed at the prospect of record-breaking flights.

The Aero Club of East Africa
Wilson Airport (PO Box 40813), Nairobi. Tel: (020) 501 772. www.aeroclubea.net

Football

More than any other, this is Kenya's national sport, played at every level from village to the hotly contested national league. The two top teams are AFC Leopards and Gor Mahia, while the national team, the Harambee Stars, have proved winners in Africa, but still have a low ranking worldwide.

The Kenya Football Federation
Nyayo Stadium, Uhuru Highway (PO Box 40234), Nairobi. Tel: (020) 201 2194. www.kff.co.ke

Golf

Golf has been popular in Kenya since the 1930s, but it is only recently that people have begun to regard the country as a suitable place for a golfing holiday. There are 6 high-quality, 18-hole courses in and around Nairobi, of which the finest, without question, is at the Windsor Golf and Country Club. This tough 7,400yd (6,750m) course has been built to international standards in hopes of attracting the top professional circuit.

The coast has two splendid courses, Nyali Beach Golf Course and Country Club, and also a fine course at Diani Beach, part of Leisure Lodge, but open to the public. In addition, there are ten courses outside Nairobi in the Central Highlands and Rift Valley areas. For more information refer to *www.kenya-golf-safaris.com*

The **Windsor Golf and Country Club** is *13km (8 miles) from Nairobi city centre, off Garden Estate Rd, PO Box 45587. Tel: (020) 856 2300. www.windsorgolfresort.com*
Muthaiga Country Club offers temporary and reciprocating membership, but it is expensive. *Tel: (020) 376 7554. www.mcc.co.ke*
Karen Country Club, with golf and other sports, is also expensive. *Tel: (020) 883 438/882/801/2. www.karencountryclub.org*
The coast courses are **Nyali** (*tel: (041) 471 589*) and **Leisure Lodge** (*tel: (040) 320 3624. www.leisurelodgeresort.com*).

Hiking

Much of the best hiking in Kenya is high altitude, with the summit of Mount Kenya as the great goal. Several other ranges, including Mount Elgon, the Aberdares and the Cheranganis offer brilliant mountain walking.

The other great way to do some serious hiking is on a walking safari through game country. There are several varieties on offer, using trucks or camels as back-up. *See also pp72–5,* or contact the **Mountain Club of Kenya**, *Wilson Airport (PO Box 45741), Nairobi. Tel: (020) 501 747. www.mck.or.ke. For planning safaris, see pp138–41.*

The 18th hole at Nyali Beach Golf Course

Sport and leisure

Horse racing

Races are held at the Nairobi Racecourse on most Sunday afternoons, except in August and September.

Jockey Club of Kenya
PO Box 40373, Nairobi.
Tel: (020) 387 3994.
www.jockeyclubofkenya.com

Nairobi Racecourse
Ngong Rd, 10km (6 miles) southwest of the city centre. Tel: (020) 566 108. Free admission to the Silver Ring.

Motor sports

The Safari Rally

One of the world's greatest motoring events and one of the toughest rallies, the Safari Rally was part of the Intercontinental Rally Challenge calendar in 2009, and was held in April.
www.motorsportkenya.com

Rhino Charge is altogether different and typifies white Kenya at play. Held

Windsurfing at Diani Beach

annually in May, in a different part of Kenya each year, Rhino Charge is a sort of 4WD version of orienteering over very rough terrain. Each team must visit ten control points over a period of ten hours and by the shortest distance possible. The event raises enormous sums for the rhino fence in the Aberdare National Park and has been held annually for the last 12 years.
www.rhinoark.org

Watersports

Diving and snorkelling

The snorkelling is superb and most coastal hotels have equipment for hire. Access to the reefs is usually by glass-bottomed boats. Be very careful not to damage the coral.

You need to be trained in order to dive. If qualified, take your certificates, or be prepared to take a test. Most of the diving here is drift diving, with a normal maximum depth of 30m (98ft) and visibility of around 25 to 35m (82 to 115ft). The preferred season is from September to April. The best sites are in the marine parks, especially in the Malindi/Watamu area. There is a park admission fee on top of the boat and equipment hire. Though all hotels tend to have a dive centre, one company, **Buccaneer**, is outstanding.

It is the only 5-star PADI LDC centre on the Kenyan coast and the only one with a PADI course director. It has bases at the Whitesands, Voyager, and Sun and Sands hotels (*www.buccaneerdiving.com*).

Fishing (deep-sea)

Kenya has some of the greatest sports-fishing grounds in the world, and a nine-month season from August to May. The main species found here include blue, black and striped marlin, swordfish, sailfish, sharks, kingfish, dorado, barracuda and wahoo. All operators are increasingly encouraging a catch-and-release policy to help conservation and scientific research.

Hemingways Resort The greatest deep-sea fishing centre in Kenya.
PO Box 267, Watamu, 25km (16 miles) south of Malindi. Tel/fax: (042) 32624/ 32256. www.hemingways.co.ke

James Adcock Fishing Ltd *Mtwapa Creek (PO Box 95693), Nyali, Mombasa. Tel: (042) 32362. www.jamesadcockfishing.com*

Malindi Sea Fishing Club *Just south of Malindi jetty. Tel: (042) 30550.*

Pemba Channel Fishing and Diving Club Based at Shimoni with trips to Kisite Island (*see p117*).
PO Box 86952, Mombasa. Tel/fax: 722 205 020/(041) 491 265. www.pembachannel.com

Fishing (freshwater)

The streams of the Aberdares, the Mau Escarpment and the Cheranganis provide excellent fly-fishing opportunities, especially for trout. Lake Victoria is an excellent centre for game-fishing with tiger fish and Nile perch among other species. With the exception of the exclusive Rusinga Island and Mfangano Island resorts

(*see pp90–91*), there are no organised facilities. You can hire equipment cheaply through the Naro Moru River Lodge (*see p73*), the Mount Kenya Safari Club (*see p69*) and Let's Go Travel Ltd.

For more information, check the **Dagoretti Trout and Salmon Flies Factory**, a major manufacturer and exporter of fly-fishing lures. Choose from an enormous range at a fraction of their Western price. Take a local guide for security in the area (*Kikuyu Rd, Nairobi. Tel: (020) 569 790*).

Swimming

There are few public swimming pools, but most good hotels have one. Do not swim in lakes and rivers, as many have bilharzia and crocodiles.

Access to the sea is easy along the coast. South from Mombasa, there is a lot of seaweed close to the shore. Never let children swim unattended as there can be strong waves and currents as well as nasties, such as sea urchins, on the bottom.

Other watersports

Windsurfing, kite-surfing, kayaking and waterskiing are available at many coastal resorts. Check at your hotel's reception desk.

Harald Geier's Windsurfing School
Surf and Safaris Ltd, Turtle Bay Beach Hotel, PO Box 168, Watamu. Tel/fax: (042) 32622/32268.

Food and drink

It comes as a surprise to find Kenya as something of a gourmet paradise. Africa as a whole is not noted for the quality of its food, but Kenya has one massive advantage – it can produce almost everything from fine beef to a wide variety of seafood, from strawberries and apples to bananas, passion fruit and papaya. The quality and range of the superb tropical fruits is the single greatest treat the country has to offer.

As each new wave of people has entered the country, they have brought their traditional foods with them. The result is an enormous range of cuisines, from traditional African fare to English pies and puddings. Swahili and Indian dishes have been absorbed as local standards, and pizza, pasta and hamburgers are coming up from behind. Meanwhile, the international tourist trade has quietly transformed standards, bringing in foreign chefs who can rival the best French kitchens. Most restaurants have at least one vegetarian option.

Food tends to come in enormous quantities – either in set meals of several courses, or on the groaning buffet tables that have become a Kenyan hallmark. These can be found in most hotels and restaurants and offer amazing value, as-much-as-you-can-eat feasts for ludicrously low prices.

Vegetarian food

Vegetarians are well catered for in Kenya, with even specialist meat or seafood restaurants such as Nairobi's Carnivore and Mombasa's Tamarind offering vegetarian options. All the eating places frequented by tourists normally include a good range of non-meat possibilities, and some, especially Indian restaurants, actually specialise in vegetarian food. At the simplest level, much local African food is totally vegetable-based, with meat being reserved for special occasions.

Prices

The catering industry in Kenya must cover the range from the migrant worker from Turkana, living on almost nothing, to the UN official attending a conference in Gigiri. The roadside stall selling roasted maize cobs and cassava chips and the gourmet restaurant of international standard often exist side by side. Most tourists never venture near the lower end of the scale.

From the top end downwards there is a very wide range of restaurants and cafés, where prices are similar to what you might pay in Europe.

In the following list of recommended restaurants, the star rating indicates the approximate cost per person per meal, not including alcohol or coffee, in Kenyan shillings:

★ under KES 1,000
★★ KES 1,000–2,000
★★★ KES 2,000–3,000
★★★★ over KES 3,000

WHERE TO EAT/DRINK

There are many excellent restaurants in Nairobi and Mombasa, but away from these centres there is often little choice. In the game parks, you have to eat at your lodge. It takes some effort to move around at night from many of the coastal resort hotels and in the smaller towns you will find one reasonable restaurant, usually in the old colonial hotel, and some fairly hygienic hotels, roadside and market stalls, serving cheap African food or fish and chips. These can be fun for an evening with a difference, but while the food is edible, you will rarely get a good meal.

The following list makes no attempt to cover every destination and also generally ignores those hotels which are already well advertised, although many of them do serve excellent food.

Nairobi
Kowloon Garden ★
Good authentic Chinese food in a typical Chinese restaurant setting.
Nginyo Towers, 2nd Floor, Koinange St, City Centre. Tel: (020) 318 885. Open: daily 11am–3.30pm & 6–10.30pm.

Bangkok ★★
Authentic Chinese cuisine, specialising in seafood – wonderful crab dishes.
Amee Arcade, Parklands Rd, Westlands. Tel: (020) 375 1312. Open: daily 11am–3pm & 6–10.30pm.

Dormans Coffee Shop ★★
Coffeehouse chain. Also serves sandwiches, pastries and smoothies.
Various locations. www.dorman.co.ke. Open: daily 7am–9pm.

Nairobi Java House ★★
Coffeehouse chain with snacks for breakfast, lunch and dinner.
Various locations. www.nairobijavahouse.com. Open: daily 7am–9pm.

Outside Inn ★★
Pub popular with sports fans on account of the big screen TV.
Karen Rd.

Pavement Club & Café ★★★
Good, varied menu including Japanese, Thai and Italian dishes. Popular with expats.
Westview Centre, Ring Rd, Westlands. Tel: (020) 444 1711. Café open: daily noon–4pm & 7–11pm. Club open: Wed–Sun 7pm–late.

Le Rustique ★★★
Charming place for lunch: local art on the walls and a pretty garden setting.
General Mathenge Dr, Westlands. Tel: (020) 375 3081. www.lerustique.co.ke. Open: Tue–Sat 9.30am–7pm, Sun 10am–6pm.

Thorn Tree Café ★★★
Bistro-style café, popular meeting place.
The Sarova Stanley, Kimathi St, City Centre.

Tel: (020) 228 830. Open: daily 6.30am–10pm.

Addis Ababa Ethiopian Restaurant ★★★★

Good authentic Ethiopian food with occasional live music.
Woodvale Grove, Westlands.
Tel: (020) 447 321.

Alan Bobbie's Bistro & Gardens ★★★★

Established in 1962, this restaurant specialises in gourmet French cuisine in an intimate setting.
24 Riverside Dr, Westlands.
Tel: (020) 444 6325.
Open: Mon–Sat noon–3pm & 7–10pm, Sun noon–3pm.

Carnivore ★★★★

Barbecued ostrich and crocodile are available, along with all the chicken, lamb, pork and beef you could possibly want.
Langata Rd, near Wilson Airport.
Tel: (020) 605 933.
www.tamarind.co.ke

Furusato Japanese Restaurant ★★★★

Best sushi in eastern Africa. Popular with expats.
Ring Rd, Parklands.
Tel: (020) 444 2508.

Haandi ★★★★

Consistently rated one of the best Indian restaurants in Kenya.
The Mall Shopping Centre, Ring Rd, Westlands.
Tel: (020) 444 8294. www. haandi-restaurants.com. Open: daily 12.30– 2.30pm & 7.30–10.30pm.

Karen Blixen Coffee Garden Restaurant ★★★★

Colonial atmosphere, and located in a beautiful garden.
365 Karen Rd.
Tel: (020) 882 138. www. blixencoffeegarden.co.ke. Open: daily 7am–10pm.

Mediterraneo ★★★★

Popular Italian restaurant with a good wine list.
Junction Shopping Centre, Ngong Rd. Tel: (020) 387 8608; Woodvale Grove, Westlands. Tel: (020) 444 7494. www. mediterraneorestaurant.co. ke. Open: daily noon–11pm.

Mercury Lounge ★★★★

Modern and spacious cocktail bar serving delectable tapas dishes.
ABC Shopping Centre, Waiyaki Way, Westlands. Tel: (020) 445 0378.

Open: Mon–Thur 12.30pm–2am & Fri–Sun 5pm–2am.

Moonflower Restaurant ★★★★

Classy grills and seafood. Live jazz music at the weekend.
Palacina Residence & Suites, Kitale Lane.
Tel: (020) 271 5517.

The Tamarind ★★★★

Very formal surroundings, popular for business lunches.
National Bank Building, Haile Selassie Ave, City Centre. Tel: (020) 225 1811.
www.tamarind.co.ke

Central Highlands

Kentrout ★★★

Great buffet lunches featuring, of course, fresh trout from the on-site farm.
In the village of Timau, 35km (22 miles) north of Nanyuki, signposted.
Tel: (062) 41016.
Open: daily noon–5pm.

Trout Tree Restaurant ★★★

Similar set-up as Kentrout, delicious three-course lunches in beautiful surroundings.
12km (7½ miles) south of

Nanyuki, signposted.
Tel: (062) 62059.
Open: daily 11am–4pm.

The coast

The vast majority of good restaurants in Mombasa and Malindi are in the resort hotels, most of which have a coffee shop and a couple of restaurants. Among those with the best food are the **Indian Ocean Beach Club** on Diani Beach and the **Nyali Beach Hotel**, Nyali.

Driftwood Beach Club ★★★

One of the best restaurants in Malindi, this place does great seafood dishes and an excellent curry lunch buffet on Sundays.
Casuarina Rd,
south of Malindi.
Tel: (042) 20155.
www.driftwoodclub.com.
Open: daily 12.30–
2.30pm & 7.30–10pm.

Galaxy Chinese Restaurant ★★★

One of the best Chinese restaurants on the coast. Very good ginger crab.
Archbishop Makarios St,

Mombasa. Tel: (041) 231
1256. Open: daily
11am–2.30pm & 6–11pm.

I Love Pizza ★★★

Long-established Italian restaurant doing excellent pizzas and seafood dishes.
Vasco da Gama Rd,
Malindi. Tel: (042) 20672.
Open: daily noon–3pm &
6.30–11.30pm.

Misono ★★★

Authentic Japanese cuisine and décor. The chefs offer the usual show while slicing and dicing your food.
Nakumatt Shopping
Centre, Nyali. Tel: (041)
471 454. Open: Mon–Sat
12.30–2.30pm &
7–10.30pm.

Surahi ★★★

Northern Indian cuisine with a good selection of vegetarian dishes.
Mtangani Rd, Malindi.
Tel: (042) 30452.

La Veranda ★★★

Good, traditional Italian food with homemade pastas and a large drinks menu.
Mwea Tabere St, behind
the Nakumatt Shopping
Centre, Nyali.
Tel: (041) 548 5452.
Open: daily 9am–late.

Ali Barbour's Cave Restaurant ★★★★

Situated inside a large coral cave, this is a unique dining experience.
North of the Diani
Shopping Centre, Diani.
Tel: (040) 320 2033.
www.alibarbours.com.
Open: daily 5pm–late.

Baby Marrow ★★★★

Rustic décor and intimate terraced setting. Excellent food and service.
Mama Ngina Rd,
Malindi. Tel: 733 542 584.
Open: daily 11am–2pm
& 6–11pm.

Jahazi Grill ★★★★

Swahili-influenced seafood cuisine in a dhow-like garden setting.
Serena Beach Hotel &
Spa, Mombasa. Tel: (020)
354 8771. Open: daily
12.30–2.30pm &
7.30–10pm.

Lorenzo's Restaurant ★★★★

Very good Italian cuisine and seafood.
Mwembe Resort,
Makaburini Rd, north
of Old Town, Malindi.
Tel: (042) 30573.
Open: daily 7–10.30pm.

The Old Man and the Sea ★★★★

Best place to eat in Malindi – very romantic setting, great service and gourmet seafood cuisine. Try the Indian Ocean seafood platter.

Vasco da Gama Rd, waterfront. Tel: (042) 31106. Open: daily 12–2.30pm & 7–11pm.

Shehnai ★★★★

Mombasa's classiest Indian restaurant serves excellent tandoori and mughlai dishes. Tasteful décor and pleasant atmosphere, although no alcohol is served.

Fatemi House, Maungano St, Mombasa. Tel: (041) 222 2847. Open: Tue–Sun noon–2pm & 7–10.30pm.

Tamarind ★★★★

Beautiful restaurant overlooking Mombasa Old Harbour. Superb cuisine specialising in seafood. It also offers *dhow* lunch and dinner cruises, which are highly recommended.

Silo Rd, Nyali. Tel: (041) 474 600. www.tamarind.com, www.tamarinddhow.com. Open: daily 12.30– 2.30pm & 7–10.30pm.

DRINKING IN KENYA

Drinking is an important part of social life in Kenya. Amongst the expatriate and European community, the 'sundowner' (an hour or so of drinks on the veranda) has become a social form and part of the way of life of many.

However, one must accept the fact that some Kenyans see alcohol as an evil import. Though most tourist areas have bars in hotels, a few places, such as the Lamu archipelago, are almost alcohol-free.

Kenyan beers are locally brewed in a wide range of styles, from traditional dark ales to Western-style lagers. Tusker Beer has received numerous awards at beer festivals around the world.

Most wines sold in Kenya come from South Africa, as indeed does a large proportion of manufactured foods. Wines available are usually very reasonably priced and come in the range of grape varieties popular in Europe and North America. However, Kenyan-produced wines are pretty well undrinkable and anyone who enjoys wine usually backs off after the first glass. But if you *must* experiment, there is a small range of Kenyan wines on sale which come from Naivasha. But you have been warned!

One can obtain the normal range of spirits, though they may be expensive. Cheap local versions are available, especially those distilled from sugar cane spirit. Some find these perfectly drinkable when mixed with fruit juices or tonics.

However, be warned to totally avoid locally made, unlabelled spirits, as they can be literally lethal and are responsible for numerous deaths.

On the other hand, Kenya is world-famous for its tea and coffee. Though the best is exported, coffee served in Kenya can still be excellent. Tea quality can be compromised by the low boiling point of water caused by the altitude.

Common African dishes

With the exception of the nomadic pastoralists who lived traditionally on blood and milk, most of the inland tribes have a diet high in carbohydrates, with plenty of vegetables and little meat or sugar. When an animal is slaughtered, every scrap is used and there are plenty of recipes for offal, blood sausages and even brains, although you rarely see these on a restaurant menu. Near the large lakes, apart from beans, fish (mainly tilapia) is the major source of protein.

On the coast, the key ingredients of typical Swahili food are fish (whether barracuda, snapper or lobster), rice, coconut and lime. To these are added a variety of spices from chillies to ginger, creating a delicious, fresh, piquant taste very similar to the food of Goa – which is directly opposite, on the far side of the Indian Ocean.

Ugali: a thick maize meal porridge, normally eaten with a vegetable stew or meat gravy. The maize crop, grown on marginal land because of population pressure, is constantly under threat because of Kenya's erratic weather patterns. In times of shortage this becomes something of a luxury item.

Nyama choma: literally burnt meat, usually goat, cooked over an open fire.

Sukuma wiki: kale, introduced by the Europeans as cattle fodder, was adopted by the locals as a cheap, nourishing source of vitamins. It often appears in restaurants as 'spinach'.

Matoke: mashed green plantains.

Irio: a vegetable mash of peas, maize and potatoes, usually served with a meat stew or tomato sauce.

Githeri: vegetable hotpot with almost everything in it – maize, red beans, potatoes, carrots, *sukuma wiki*, tomatoes, onions, and, sometimes, meat!

Villagers hard at work crushing grain in the traditional way

Hotels and accommodation

Kenya has a wide range of accommodation from glorious luxury hotels to sleazy tin shacks and brothels with a couple of long-stay rooms. Most of the best are owned by a handful of chains, such as Fairmont, Sarova and Serena, who all have a variety of Nairobi hotels, coastal resorts and game lodges.

Prices for quality hotels are normally listed in US dollars, with a 'resident' and a 'non-resident' rate (*see* Prices, *p185*). While the package operators negotiate substantial discounts, rack rates for non-residents are equivalent to those in the West. This may be just, but with many more affordable 3-star hotels currently upgrading, there is a dearth of decent mid-range accommodation for independent travellers.

The fullest list of hotels in the country can be found in *What's On* magazine.

Business hotels

Nairobi has plenty of excellent 5-star hotels, run by the main chains, which double up to cater for international business trade.

In Mombasa, most businessmen stay in the resort hotels in nearby Nyali Beach. All have a full range of services. Expect to pay upwards of US$150 per night.

CENTRAL BOOKING

Bush Homes of East Africa
Upmarket holiday accommodation.
Tel: (020) 600 457.
www.bush-homes.co.ke

Heritage Hotels
For Intrepids Safari Camps.
Tel: (020) 444 6651/7929.
www.heritage-eastafrica.com

Fairmont Hotels
Generally luxury locations, Nairobi and Safari.
Tel: (020) 216 940.
www.fairmont.com

Sarova Hotels
Nairobi, coast, national parks.
Tel: (020) 276 7000.
www.sarovahotels.com

Serena Hotels
Biggest group. Fine hotels and lodges.
Tel: (020) 284 2333.
www.serenahotels.com

Sopa Lodges
Lodges in Kenya and Tanzania.
Tel: (020) 375 0235.
www.sopalodges.com

Wilderness Lodges
Formerly Block Hotels.
Tel: (020) 523 329.
www.wildernesslodges.co.ke

Mid-range and old colonial hotels

Nairobi is the only city with a reasonable range of good quality, affordable hotels. The best are the **Fairview**, the **Jacaranda**, the **Boulevard** and the **Holiday Inn Nairobi**. In Mombasa, there is only one real contender, the **Castle Royal Hotel**.

Elsewhere, every town across the country has one old colonial hotel. In many instances, it is still the finest on offer. With the odd exception, such as the luxurious (and expensive) **Norfolk Hotel** in Nairobi, most have sunk back into atmospheric decay, but they are usually spotlessly clean and perfectly comfortable. Most are privately owned and there is no central listing, but ask any local. Many 3-star establishments cater primarily for locals, so they have not bothered with non-resident rates. Expect to pay US$70–100 a night.

Cheap and cheerful

There is at least one cheap hotel in even the tiniest of towns, but quality ranges from spartan to dire. Always ask to check the room before booking in.

Nairobi has a good Youth Hostel, YMCA and YWCA and several clean, comfortable budget hotels.

On the coast, there are one or two good cheap hotels in central Mombasa, but most budget travellers head for Tiwi Beach, which has excellent self-catering accommodation.

There are no budget hotels in wildlife parks, but there are usually *bandas*, which can be a variety of simple, but usually adequate accommodation, sometimes beautifully designed. Kenya Wildlife Service (*see p138*) produces an up-to-date *banda* list.

Hotels on the coast

Due to fluctuating trade in recent years, some hotels, particularly on the coast, have started to close in low season. Check with your travel agent or with central hotel booking.

Out-of-town coastal resorts

From Malindi, right down to the southern end of Diani Beach, more and more resort hotels have sprung up. Most are 4- or 5-star and, with the exception of a few early constructions, have similar, attractive architecture – a large central building with *makute* (coconut) thatch, surrounded by comfortable cottages spread out across landscaped gardens. They all have beach frontage and swimming pools and offer a variety of entertainments from tribal dancing to watersports. Most are geared towards the package trade and all-in prices, though the operators are very competitive.

Check before booking who the main operators are, as the different nationalities tend to book into different hotels (one for the Germans, one for the Italians, etc). The occasional lost soul can spend a lonely holiday, unable to communicate with anyone round him or her. Prices are about the same as in the game lodges.

Game lodges

All Kenya's main game parks offer a variety of upmarket lodges. The area in and around Masai Mara, for example, has about 30 lodges and camps. Those within the gates may seem more convenient, as staying outside the park may involve an hour's bumpy drive before you get into the reserve. On the other hand, many lodges on the fringes have created private game sanctuaries which act as extensions of the park proper and have one or two real bonuses. On private land, you can go out on guided walks or rides and night drives. Many of the lodges have also created artificial waterholes and salt licks and even bait for leopards, so that you have unparalleled game viewing from the comfort of the veranda.

Most of the lodges are low, expansive buildings set in bright flower gardens. As you are confined within the lodge in the evening they do their best to arrange for a wide variety of meals and entertainments, from filmshows to the ubiquitous Maasai dancers. You spend the midday heat back at base, so choose a lodge with a swimming pool.

For this level of accommodation expect to pay upwards of US$200 a day (high season) or US$150 (low season), double bed or twin sharing.

Permanent tented camps

In many ways, these tented camps are very similar to the game lodges and cost as much. They were designed to cater for those who believe that a real safari meant sleeping under canvas. However, they are a long way from the dream of a night under the stars in the middle of nowhere. In most, the tents have double 'skins' to protect you from extremes of the weather. They also have soft beds, electric light and fully fitted private bathrooms. The tents are all on permanent pitches in landscaped grounds, there is always at least one bar, a restaurant and often a pool.

Private ranches

Increasingly, private ranches and conservation areas are being opened up for visitors. One example is Lewa Wildlife Conservancy.

Located about 40km (25 miles) north of Nanyuki, Lewa is a former cattle ranch which is now a safe haven for endangered black rhino and Grevy's zebra. Lewa Safari Camp is not dissimilar to other high-class permanent tented camps. Lewa House and Wilderness Trails, on the other hand, are both houses, where very small groups can live as 'part of the family'. Standards are luxurious, but such personalised treatment does not come cheap.

There is a good road to Lewa from Nairobi, but the majority of guests fly into one of two private airstrips.

In the following list of recommended accommodation, the star rating indicates the approximate cost per room per night. The price guide here has taken current pricing and converted it to Kenyan shillings (approximately 75 shillings to the US dollar).

★   under KES 3,500

★★   KES 3,500–10,000

★★★   KES 10,000–25,000

★★★★ over KES 25,000

Nairobi

Hotel Kipepeo ★

Fairly new budget hotel with good security.

River Rd, City Centre.

Tel: (020) 313 571.

www.hotelkipepeo.com

Milimani Backpackers ★

Friendly, budget option.

Milimani Rd, Nairobi Hill. Tel: (020) 234 3920.

www.milimanibackpackers. com

Gigiri Homestead ★★

Pleasant rooms in a friendly home.

54 United Nations Crescent, Gigiri.

Tel: (020) 354 4189.

www.gigirihomestead.com

Fairview ★★★

Very popular, good value, friendly family-run hotel.

Bishops Rd, Nairobi Hill.

Tel: (020) 288 1000.

www.fairviewkenya.com

The Sarova Stanley ★★★

Centrally located, this recently renovated hotel has been around since 1902.

Kimathi St, City Centre.

Tel: (020) 271 4444.

www.sarovahotels.com

Giraffe Manor ★★★★

This English-style red brick country house is pure luxury.

Koitobos Rd, Langata.

Tel: (020) 251 3166, (020) 891 078.

www.giraffemanor.com

Ngong House ★★★★

With beautiful views of the Ngong Hills and very good food, this place is a hidden gem.

Induvo Lane, Karen.

Tel: (020) 891 856.

www.ngonghouse.com

The Norfolk Hotel ★★★★

Built in 1904, the Norfolk is one of Nairobi's original buildings.

Harry Thuku Rd, Nairobi.

Tel: (020) 226 5000.

www.fairmont.com

The Rift Valley

Kembu Cottages and Campsite ★★

En-suite cottages, campsites, rooms and a treehouse all on a large friendly working farm.

Nakuru.

Tel: (0722) 361 102.

www.kembu.com

Sarova Lion Hill Game Lodge ★★★

En-suite chalet-style rooms with lovely views.

Lake Nakuru National Park. Tel: (051) 208 5455.

www.sarovahotels.com

Governors' Camp ★★★★

Luxury tents ideally situated by the Mara River for game viewing.

Masai Mara National Reserve.

Tel: (020) 273 4000.

www.governorscamp.com

Kicheche Mara Camp ★★★★

Luxury en-suite tents in an idyllic bush setting.

Greater Mara, Aitong Plains, northern Koiyaki Lemek region.

Tel: (020) 890 358.

www.kicheche.com

The Central Highlands

Mountain Rock Lodge ★★

The reputable lodge arranges treks up Mount Kenya.

Mount Kenya Biosphere Reserve, Nanyuki.

Tel: (020) 224 2133.

www.mountainrockkenya. com

The Ark ★★★

Uniquely shaped tree-lodge, located in the centre of the park.

Aberdare National Park.

Tel: (020) 216 940.

www.fairmont.com

Blue Posts Hotel ★★★
Built in 1908, this lodge is still the most popular hotel and restaurant in the area.
Muranga Rd, Thika.
Tel: (067) 22241.

Naro Moru River Lodge ★★★
With a variety of accommodation, the lodge organises treks up Mount Kenya.
Mount Kenya Biosphere Reserve, Naro Moru.
Tel: (020) 444 3357.
www.alliancehotels.com

Outspan Hotel ★★★
Built in 1927, this historic hotel has spacious rooms and is set in well-cared-for gardens.
Baden Powell Rd, Nyeri.
Tel: (061) 203 2424. www.
aberdaresafarihotels.com

Treetops ★★★
This lodge-on-stilts has small cabins with shared bathroom facilities and great views of the wildlife at the waterholes below.
Aberdare National Park.
Tel: (061) 203 4914. www.
aberdaresafarihotels.com

Lewa Downs ★★★★
Comfortable en-suite cottages on a private game park.

Lewa Wildlife Conservancy, Isiolo.
Tel: (020) 600 457. www.
bush-and-beyond.com

Mount Kenya Safari Club ★★★★
Recently renovated, this luxurious and exclusive hotel is arranged as cottages.
Mount Kenya Biosphere Reserve, Nanyuki.
Tel: (020) 221 6940.
www.fairmont.com

Western Kenya
Kericho Tea Hotel ★★
The best option when staying in Kericho, and right next to the tea plantations.
Moi Highway, Kericho.
Tel: (052) 30004.

Kiboko Bay Resort ★★★
Friendly, lakeside resort with a nice restaurant.
Kisumu. Tel: (057) 202 5510. www.kibokobay.com

Mfangano Island Camp ★★★★
The only luxury accommodation in the area, this camp matches the high standards of other Governors' Camps.
Mfangano Island.
Tel: (020) 273 4000.
www.governorscamp.com

Rusinga Island Lodge ★★★★
Pretty cottages overlooking the lake. Accessed by private charter plane.
Rusinga Island.
Tel: (020) 253 1314.
www.rusinga.com

The Coast
Castle Royal Hotel ★★
Built in 1909, this renovated colonial hotel has 60 en-suite rooms, all air-conditioned.
Moi Ave, Mombasa.
Tel: (041) 222 2682.

Kenya Bay Beach Hotel ★★
Friendly, good value hotel with watersport activities available.
Bamburi Beach.
Tel: (041) 548 7600.
www.kenyabay.com

Lotus Hotel ★★
Good value hotel near Old Town Mombasa.
Cathedral Lane, Mombasa.
Tel: (041) 231 3207.
www.lotushotelkenya.com

Coral Cove Cottages ★★★
Comfortable self-catering cottages on the beach.
Tiwi Beach.
Tel: (040) 330 0010. www.
coralcove.tiwibeach.com

Driftwood Beach Club ★★★

Well-established hotel with a good restaurant.
Malindi.
Tel: (042) 212 0155.
www.driftwoodclub.com

Lamu House ★★★

Lovely Swahili-style terraced rooms.
Kenyatta Ave, Lamu town. Tel: (042) 633 491.
www.lamuhouse.com

Peponi's ★★★

Beachfront hotel with comfortable cottages, and an excellent restaurant.
Shela Beach, Lamu.
Tel: (042) 463 3421.
www.peponi-lamu.com

The Sands at Nomad ★★★

Boutique hotel with Swahili-influenced rooms and 12 luxurious suites.
Diani Beach.
Tel: 724 262 426. www.
thesandsatnomad.com

Funzi Keys ★★★★

Perfect for a romantic honeymoon, with four-poster beds and a private beach.
Funzi Island, south of Msambweni.
Tel: (0733) 900 582.
www.thefunzikeys.com

Hemingways ★★★★

Famous fishing club hotel with a very good restaurant.
Watamu.
Tel: (042) 233 2624.
www.hemingways.co.ke

Voyager Beach Resort ★★★★

Very popular package holiday resort.
Nyali Beach.
Tel: (020) 444 6651. www.
heritage-eastafrica.com

The North

Samburu Game Lodge ★★★

This lodge was the first in the reserve and is still a popular choice.
Samburu National Reserve.
Tel: (020) 532 329.

Elephant Watch Safari Camp ★★★★

Eco-conscious luxury tented camp.
Samburu National Reserve.
Tel: (020) 891 112. www.
elephantwatchsafaris.com

Loisaba Wilderness ★★★★

Exclusive private wildlife lodge.
Laikipia Plateau.
Tel: (062) 31072.
www.loisaba.com

Southern Kenya

Kilaguni Serena Safari Lodge ★★★

Comfortable rooms and an abundance of wildlife.
Tsavo West National Park.
Tel: (045) 340 000.
www.serenahotels.com

Ngulia Safari Lodge ★★★

Popular with birdwatchers, this simple lodge overlooks the Ngulia Rhino Sanctuary.
Tsavo West National Park.
Tel: (041) 471 861.
www.safari-hotels.com

Satao Camp ★★★

Permanent tented camp by a waterhole popular with lions, hippos, elephants and zebras.
Tsavo East National Park.
Tel: (041) 243 4600.
www.sataocamp.com

Amboseli Serena Safari Lodge ★★★★

Blending harmoniously with the landscape, this lodge offers 96 renovated rooms.
Amboseli National Park.
Tel: (045) 622 361.
www.serenahotels.com

Finch Hattons ★★★★

Award-winning luxury tented camp.
Tsavo West National Park.
Tel: (020) 553 237.
www.finchhattons.com

Practical guide

Arriving by air

Nairobi is the main air travel centre for East Africa, with regular scheduled flights by many airlines from around the world and is the best place in Africa for discounted tickets. Some international scheduled services fly into Mombasa airport, but this is mainly used by the charter companies. The state airline, Kenya Airways, runs regular services to some 30 destinations worldwide.

Airlines

Whether travelling from Europe or North America, the flight into Nairobi will probably be with one of the three most convenient airlines.

British Airways via London Heathrow
Kenya Airways via London or Amsterdam
KLM via Amsterdam

Other airlines, less frequent, operate as follows:

Brussels Airlines from UK via Brussels
Egypt Air from London via Cairo
Emirates from several UK airports via Dubai
Ethiopian Airlines from UK via Addis Ababa
Qatar Airways from UK via Doha
Turkish Arlines from UK via Istanbul
Virgin Atlantic two flights a day from London

As you will book in a variety of possible ways and increasingly online, no outward contacts are given. However, airline contact numbers in Nairobi are as follows:

British Airways *Tel: (020) 327 7246*
Egypt Air *Tel: (020) 226 821/3*
Emirates *Tel: (020) 329 000*
Gulf Air *Tel: (020) 241 123/8*
Kenya Airways and **KLM** *Tel: (020) 320 74747*
Virgin Atlantic *Tel: (0729) 880 002 (mobile)*

Within Kenya, the two main scheduled internal airlines are:

Air Kenya *Tel: (020) 501 601; 605 745*
Safari Link *Tel: (020) 600 777*
Mombasa Air Safari *Tel: (041) 343 3061*

Airports
Nairobi-Jomo Kenyatta International
A duty-free shop is available on arrival and departure, and there is 24-hour banking in the arrivals hall. Kenya Airways buses run to and from the City Terminal on Loita Street; most local hotels organise airport transfers; and there are plenty of taxis.
Off Mombasa Rd, PO Box 19001, 18km (11 miles) southeast of the city centre. Tel: (020) 661 1000.

Wilson Airport Located between the city and Nairobi National Park, the airport deals with most of the light aircraft movements. It claims to be the busiest airport in Africa (*tel: (020) 501 943*).

Mobasa-Moi International There are 24-hour banking and duty-free facilities available on arrival and departure. Many offices open only for flights. There is a regular public bus into the city, but most tourist hotels are not on Mombasa island. Ask your hotel for transport or take a taxi.
Off Nairobi Rd, PO Box 98498, 13km (8 miles) west of the city centre (tel: (041) 343 3211).

Airport taxes/visas

Taxes and visa charges change fairly frequently. It is most important that you check this information with your travel agent. It is possible in most cases to obtain your tourist visa (if you need one – *see pp176–7*) on arrival, although, after a long journey, it can be a trying business. Payment must be in hard currency.

Customs

Currency There is no limit on the amount of foreign currency you can bring in or take out. It is illegal to import or export Kenyan shillings. You can reconvert leftover cash if you have exchange receipts to cover the amount.
Drugs There are very stiff penalties for drug dealing. If you take drugs for medical purposes, it's best to take a copy of your prescription with you.
Duty-free allowances You may bring into Kenya: 227g (8 oz) of tobacco, or 200 cigarettes, or 50 cigars; 1 litre (2 pints) of alcohol (wine or spirits) per person; and 0.6 litres (1.2 pints) of perfume.

Arriving by land

Kenya has land borders with Tanzania, Uganda, Sudan, Ethiopia and Somalia, officially open, but overland travel through southern Sudan and Somalia is inadvisable. To bring in your own vehicle, you will need a Carnet (available through the AA) to avoid paying duty and you will need to buy local insurance on arrival in the first major town. An International Authorisation Permit, issued free for the first seven days, is also required. Regulations change constantly; be sure to check with your travel agent.

Arriving by sea

The **Africa Shipping Corporation** sometimes runs a service between Mombasa and Zanzibar (*tel: (011) 315 178*). Ask the local travel agents.

Camping

Kenya has raised camping to an art form, with every possible variation from a pup tent to a luxury permanent camp. There are also plenty of independent campsites. Most are fairly basic, however, and you have to take in everything from firewood to drinking water. Camping outside the designated areas is highly inadvisable. One or two car hire companies will supply a safari vehicle complete with camping equipment, but it is almost as cheap, and much easier, to take one of the camping safaris offered by every tour operator in the country.

Children

See pp156–7.

Climate

Kenya is on the equator but its altitudes and terrain vary enormously. Temperatures remain fairly stable all year round, as do the hours of daylight (roughly 6am to 6.30pm), but there are several distinct climatic regions.

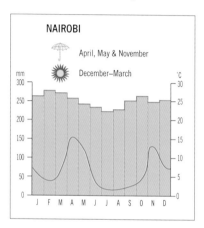

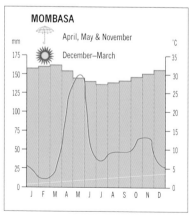

WEATHER CONVERSION CHART

25.4mm = 1 inch
°F = 1.8 × °C + 32

The coast is always hot and often humid, while the highlands are warm during the day and chilly at night. Nairobi's 25°C during the day represents 77°F, whereas Mombasa at 30°C+ represents 86°F+. Western Kenya tends to be warm and relatively wet all year round, while the semi-desert lands of the far north are always very hot and dry.

There are two rainy seasons: the Short Rains in November and December and the Long Rains in April and May. There is a dismal season, though by no means 'winter', in July and August, when the skies around Nairobi, especially, are almost permanently cloudy.

Conversion tables

See opposite.
Clothes and shoe sizes in Kenya generally follow the standard sizes used in the UK.

Crime

See p38.

Documents

All visitors must have a passport with at least three months validity and an onward ticket or proof of funds. Visas are currently required by everyone except residents of east African countries, but do check, as rules change. Current price per visitor is US$25, or £20 sterling, for three months. It is possible to obtain visas on arrival (hard currency only), but the process is chaotic and wearisome after a long journey and not the best introduction to Kenya.

If you apply in advance, allow ample time as applications may take up to six weeks.

Visa extensions are possible in Nairobi, at the Immigration Office (*Nyayo House, on the corner of Uhuru Highway and Kenyatta Avenue. Tel: (020) 332 110*) and also at Mombasa Immigration Office (*Tel: (041) 311 745*). Allow a morning.

Electricity

240 volts with three-square-pin plugs. The power supply is generally reliable although there are occasional failures and some rationing due to excess demand or storms. Most hotels and lodges have their own generators, but a torch is always useful, and essential if camping.

Kenyan Embassies and High Commissions worldwide

Australia
Level 3, Manpower Building, 33–35 Ainslie Place, Civic Square, Canberra ACT 2601. Tel: (026) 247 4788. www.kenya.asn.au

Canada
Ste 600, 415 Laurier Ave East, Ottawa. Tel: (0613) 563 1773. www.kenyahighcommission.ca

France
3 Rue Freycinet, 75016 Paris. Tel: (1) 47 20 44 41. www.kenyaembassyparis.org

Germany
Markgrafen Str 63, Berlin. Tel: (030) 259 2660. www.embassy-of-kenya.de

CONVERSION TABLE

FROM	TO	MULTIPLY BY
Inches	Centimetres	2.54
Feet	Metres	0.3048
Yards	Metres	0.9144
Miles	Kilometres	1.6090
Acres	Hectares	0.4047
Gallons	Litres	4.5460
Ounces	Grams	28.35
Pounds	Grams	453.6
Pounds	Kilograms	0.4536
Tons	Tonnes	1.0160

To convert back, for example from centimetres to inches, divide by the number in the third column.

UK
45 Portland Place, London W1B 1AS. Tel: (020) 7636 2371. www.kenyahighcommission.net

USA
2249 R St NW, Washington, DC 20008. Tel: (202) 387 6101. www.kenyaembassy.com

Foreign Embassies and Consulates in Nairobi

Australia
New Chancery, Riverside Drive, PO Box 39341. Tel: (020) 444 5034/9. www.kenya.embassy.gov.au

Canada
Comcraft House, Haile Selassie Ave, PO Box 1013-00621. Tel: (020) 366 3000. www.kenya.gc.ca

Ireland
O'Washika Road, Lavington, PO Box 39659. Tel: (020) 562 615.

UK
PO Box 30465-00100. Tel: (020) 284 4000. www.ukinkenya.fco.gov.uk

Practical guide

USA
United Nations Ave, PO Box 606,
Village Market 00621.
Tel: (020) 363 6000.
http://nairobi.usembassy.gov

Emergency telephone numbers

The emergency number is *999*. But be aware that apart from the police, who may or may not respond, emergency services such as ambulance and fire brigade are almost non-existent. Better to have phone numbers of friends or other contacts who can help you in an emergency.

Getting around independently
By air

There is a wide network of domestic flights operating from Moi International in Mombasa (*see pp174–5*) and Wilson Airport, Nairobi. Malindi and Kisumu also have small airports and most other towns and major game parks have airstrips. Most tour operators offer flying options. Ticket prices are very reasonable and if you are in a group it will cost little more to charter the plane yourself.

The main local airports are:
Wilson Airport *Langata Road (PO Box 19011), Nairobi, 5km (3 miles) south of the city centre.*
Moi International *See pp175.*
Kisumu Airport *Nyerere Road (PO Box 12).*
Malindi Airport *Mombasa Road (PO Box 67).*
In addition, Kenya has over 400 airstrips. Scheduled internal flights

connect Nairobi with Mombasa, Lamu, Malindi, Kisumu and all major parks and reserves.
Carriers are: **Air Kenya**, *tel: (020) 501 601/605 745* and **Safari Link**, *tel: (020) 600 777.*
Both operate from Wilson Airport while **Kenya Airways** does some internal routes for Jomo Kenyatta International Airport.

Air charter companies
There are about 15 air charter companies in Kenya, mostly fixed wing and mostly operating from Wilson Airport.
Nairobi fixed wing charter companies:
African Sky Charters (*tel: (020) 601 467*).
Air Adventures Kenya Ltd (*tel: (020) 884 258*).
Boskovic Air Charters (*tel: (020) 606 364*).
East African Air Charter (*tel: (020) 603 858*).
Phoenix Air Safaris (*tel: (020) 572 373*).
Queensway Air Service (*tel: (020) 608 619*).
Safari Link Aviation (*tel: (020) 600 039*).
Yellow Wings Air Service (*tel: (020) 606 313*).

By rail
With privatisation of the rail system, things should improve over the coming years (*see p144*).

By road and car hire
If you are unused to African driving, seriously consider hiring a car with a driver. Generally the standard of driving

is dreadful, the roads are terrible and if you are not used to driving on the left, that might be the last straw.

A 4WD vehicle may be essential, depending on where you are going. Take advice. There are scores of companies in the Yellow Pages, including well-known names. These might be most reliable, but not exclusively.

Avis *Koinange St. Tel: (020) 336 703/704.*
Budget *Hilton Hotel. Tel: (020) 222 3581.*
Concorde Car Hire *Sarit Centre. Tel: (020) 379 3304.*
Hertz *Mbingu St. Tel: (020) 311 143.*
National *Woodland Grove, Westlands. Tel: (020) 440 333/335.*

Driving

Driving is on the left, giving way to traffic coming in from the right at roundabouts. Your national licence is valid for 90 days, but an international one would be better. Fuel is available in all towns and at many game lodges, but it is advisable to carry a jerry can if heading out of town. Try to be off the road by dark, both for security and because of the many lethal vehicles with no lights.

Though there are some good roads, for example, much of the Nairobi to Mombasa road, most are extremely poor. Journeys are usually much slower and more tiring than you would expect and you will almost inevitably have to cope with breakdowns, punctures and even getting stuck. Make sure you have

a good set of tools, a good spare tyre (preferably two) and a new inner tube as well. The locals are usually helpful, for a price, and there is someone in every village to mend the punctures. On isolated roads or in the parks, report in to the ranger or police station so that someone knows where you are.

Hitchhiking

Do not hitch. It is possible, but is very dangerous these days. The best way to find a lift is to ask around the hotels and campsites. Expect to split petrol costs.

Health

AIDS

HIV/AIDS is endemic in Kenya, especially amongst the sexually active population. This is no reason to be alarmed as you will only be at risk if you have unprotected sex or use contaminated needles. Avoid the temptations of the huge numbers of prostitutes and always use a condom. It's best to avoid casual sex totally. Take a pack of sterile needles and insist on using them if you need an injection. If you need a blood transfusion, throw yourself on the mercy of your friends or contact your embassy. Some have lists of 'clean' donors and even blood banks.

Altitude sickness

This is only a problem on high altitude hikes, such as the trek up Mount Kenya. *See pp72–5.*

Bilharzia

This small, unpleasant worm uses freshwater snails as its intermediate host. You should be safe in very cold or fast-flowing water, but to be safe, stay out of all fresh water except swimming pools. If you do get wet, towel off briskly within a few minutes. If you feel you have been at risk, get a simple test done at your nearest tropical diseases unit. Treatment is easy if the disease is caught in time.

Cuts and scratches

These minor scrapes can easily become infected, septic and even ulcerous in the tropics. Clean them out thoroughly, apply antiseptic ointment and keep them covered up. If you see signs of infection, take antibiotics.

Inoculations

A yellow fever vaccination is mandatory if travelling from an infected area and advisable anyway. Also recommended: typhoid, polio, tetanus and hepatitis A inoculation. Your GP will give you best current advice. Allow two months for a full set.

Hospitals and doctors

For routine treatments, the quality of healthcare is good. Most doctors have trained or spent some time working in the West. All staff speak English and you can usually find someone who speaks French, German or Italian. For anything more complicated, the best hospitals in the country are:

Nairobi Hospital *Argwings Kodhek Road, Nairobi. Tel: (020) 284 5000. www.nairobihospital.org*
The Aga Khan Hospital *3rd Ave, Parklands, Nairobi. Tel: (020) 374 2531. www.agakahnhospitals.org*
The Aga Khan Hospital *Vanga Road, Mombasa. Tel: (041) 222 7710.*

There are numerous other hospitals listed in *What's On* magazine. Private clinics are generally better stocked with drugs and equipment and will be more comfortable if you have to stay in. Make sure your travel insurance will cover the costs and, if necessary, will cover a medivac flight home.

Many rural hospitals are basic clinics. If in doubt, contact the local mission. If planning to stray off the beaten track, take out temporary membership of the Amref Flying Doctor Service, Wilson Airport *(tel: (+254) 20 601 594/602 495; mobile: (+254) 722205 084).*

For emergencies, contact **AMREF** (24 hour control. *Tel: (+254) 20 315 454; mobile: (+254) 733628422; satellite phone: (+873) 76231 5580. www.amref.org).*

Malaria

Malaria can be a killer. Prescribed dosages of anti-malarial tablets must be taken for two weeks before arrival, during your stay and for two weeks after departure. Use repellents and mosquito nets to avoid being bitten. Malaria is carried only by the female anopheles mosquito, which comes out at night.

Local malaria may have developed immunity to the most common anti-malarial drug, chloroquine, so it should be taken alongside one of the other drugs, or replaced by one of the newer substitutes. Get up-to-date advice from a specialist travel clinic or malaria hotline. If you show flu-like symptoms at any time, up to six months after your return home, ask your GP for a malaria test.

Stomach bugs

Tourist Kenya is a pretty hygienic place and there is little likelihood of getting a bug. Wash your hands before touching food and do not eat in obviously dirty establishments or touch food that has been left lying around. Always drink bottled mineral water and ask for drinks without ice. If you do get caught, try to sweat it out for 24 hours, eating nothing and drinking lots, particularly drinks with salt and sugar in them. The chief danger is from dehydration. If you need to keep on the move, you should keep a good stock of effective anti-diarrhoea medication with you. If the problem

Camping is one of the most exciting ways to feel the true call of the bush

persists for more than 48 hours, consult a doctor.

Sunburn and heatstroke

There is a huge temptation to spend every daylight hour on the beach or in the cooler highlands and forget you are on the equator.

The sun here is fierce. Always wear a hat, don't spend too long out in any one sitting and use a high-factor sunblock. If you do get burned, use huge amounts of aftersun cream. Heatstroke occurs when the body's cooling system is strained so far that it breaks down, causing the body temperature to rise uncontrollably. If this happens, get the sufferer into a cold bath immediately and call for medical help.

Rabies

Unless you are planning to handle animals, an inoculation against rabies should be unnecessary. Should you have the misfortune to be bitten, however, you must start a course of treatment immediately. If you wait for symptoms to appear, it is too late.

Insurance

Good travel insurance is absolutely necessary. Most importantly, you should have good, all-purpose medical cover, including medivac facilities. In addition, it should cover third-party liability, legal assistance, loss of personal possessions (including cash, traveller's cheques and documents) and should contain some

Nairobi headquarters of *The Nation* media group

facility for cancellation and delay in your travel arrangements. If you are planning to take part in any adventure sports, e.g. diving and climbing, check that your policy will cover you (most won't), and, if necessary, get an extension. Travel insurance does not normally cover you for liability arising from motor accidents; this requires an extra top-up policy.

Language

Each of Kenya's many tribes has its own language but Swahili is the official language of government. Strictly speaking, it is Kiswahili that is used. This is the inland dialect of the original language and, although they can understand it easily enough, the Swahili people of the coast pour scorn on what they see as a bastard offshoot of their Swahili.

You will almost always find someone who speaks English wherever you are and if you don't, the chances are you are in a remote tribal location with people who can't speak Swahili either! On the coast, many resorts will have German and Italian speakers on the staff and there will usually be someone nearby with at least a smattering of French or Spanish. Inland, you are less likely to find such a range of languages on offer.

Survival is easy, but it is considered good manners to learn at least a few words of greeting in Swahili, which can add to the enjoyment of your holiday. The language is written phonetically, so the most obvious pronunciation is correct. There are plenty of good Swahili phrase books and language CDs for those who wish to learn more than is given here.

Useful Swahili words

Welcome	Karibu
Hello	Jambo
How are you?	Habari?
Very well	Mzuri sana
Goodbye	Kwaheri/
(plural)	Kwaherini
Please	Tafhadali
Thank you	Asante
Thank you very much	Asante sana
Yes	Ndiyo
No	Hapana
Sir	Bwana
Madam	Mama
OK	Sawa sawa
I don't understand	Sielewi
Do you speak English?	Unasema Kingereza?
Excuse me	Samahani
No problem	Hakuna matata
Food	Chakula
Doctor	Daktari
How much?	Bei gani?
Money	Pesa

Glossary of common terms

Soldier/watchman	Askari
Small dwelling	Banda
Village	Boma
Tea	Chai
Small shop	Duka
Village	Manyatta
Passenger vehicle	Matatu
Tribal warrior(s)	Morani
Dirt road	Murram
White person	Mzungu
Roast meat	Nyama choma
Maize meal	Posho
Any journey	Safari
Smallholding	Shamba

Internet

Kenya has certainly not been left behind by the Internet revolution. Almost all good hotels in larger towns will offer a business facility, with a battery of computers giving Internet access. In addition, good business hotels in Nairobi offer wireless broadband connection.

Lost property

The hotels usually have a lost property department, but there are no official facilities in the country. Try the police or contact *The Nation* newspaper, who run a finding service through their Sunday edition. Your chances of recovering your possessions, however, are slim.

Maps

Bartholomews, Macmillan and Nelles all do good country maps for Kenya. There is an excellent 1:50,000 annotated map of Mount Kenya by Andrew Wielochowski and Mark Savage. These are all available in good bookshops, both in Kenya and abroad. Other than that, most local maps tend to be out of date and, therefore, you would do better to stick to the maps in this book. The new Jacana maps, presently available for Mara Triangle, Masai Mara, Amboseli, Lewa, Il Ngwesi (and some popular locations in Tanzania), are all excellent and are being extended to all of the major National Parks and Reserves.

Media

There are three English language daily newspapers, *The Nation*, *The People* and *The Standard*. The biggest and most useful is *The Nation*. A wide range of foreign papers is available a few days late in Nairobi and Mombasa. The main English language radio station and the single nationwide TV station are both run by the government-owned Kenya Broadcasting Corporation. DSTV Satellite TV is now available where there is an electricity supply and many hotels have it installed.

Money matters
Currency

The unit of currency is the Kenya shilling (KES), divided into 100 cents. There are 10, 20, 50, 100, 200 and 500 shilling notes; and 5, 10 and 50 cent and 1 and 5 shilling coins. Changing large denomination notes is difficult. *Also see* Customs *on p175*.

Exchange facilities

Most banks in Nairobi and Mombasa, and at least one in the smaller towns, will handle foreign exchange. Rates are standard, but the commission varies, as does the amount of red tape. Barclays and Standard Chartered banks are found in most places.

Banking hours are usually Monday to Friday 9am to 2pm, and on the first and last Saturday of each month, 9am to 11am. The Nairobi International and Mombasa airport exchange desks are open 24 hours a day.

Most tourist hotels and lodges will also exchange money for their guests, although some of the smaller ones may well have an upper limit of around US$100.

In Nairobi there are over 30 Foreign Exchange Bureaux (Forex), usually conveniently located in shopping areas. Rates are posted daily in newspapers.

Cheques and credit cards

Thomas Cook Traveller's Cheques are readily accepted; they should preferably be denominated in US dollars, as these are easiest to use.

Credit cards are accepted by all good hotels and most upmarket restaurants and shops. The most widely recognised are Visa and MasterCard. ATMs now exist at most banks and in all shopping malls.

Prices

Several years ago, the Kenyan government introduced separate non-resident rates, to be paid in hard currency, for all good hotels and organised safaris. Most companies took the opportunity to raise their prices dramatically. At the same time, a two-tier system was set up for museums and game parks. Most museums now charge foreigners double. Visitors must realise that local Kenyans working full-time may receive the equivalent of only £50–60 per month. Once outside this system and with the exception of car hire, Kenya is pretty cheap.

Public holidays

1 January New Year's Day
March/April Good Friday, Easter Monday
1 May Labour Day
1 June Madaraka Day (anniversary of self-government)
10 October Moi Day (anniversary of Moi's inauguration)
20 October Kenyatta Day (anniversary of Kenyatta's arrest)
12 December Jamhuri Day (anniversary of independence)
25 December Christmas Day
26 December Boxing Day
Id-ul-Fitr Muslim celebration of the end of Ramadan (variable from year to year)

Malindi Mosque

National parks and reserves

Kenya has over 40 national parks and reserves, collectively an area bigger than Switzerland. Although reserves are run by local councils, even the Masai Mara, national parks are all under the auspices of the Kenya Wildlife Service. All parks are open from 6am to 6pm, and you must be either out of the park or in camp by curfew. Only a few (those without large predators) will allow you in on foot, and in all parks your vehicle must be registered in Kenya.

Opening hours

These are listed under the relevant sections throughout this book.

Pharmacies

There are numerous pharmacies in Nairobi and Mombasa and at least one in each small town. Many open from 8am to 8pm and at least one will stay open late each evening. An out-of-hours contact number should be posted in the window and is published in *The Nation* newspaper and *What's On* magazine.

Places of worship

Kenya is literally teeming with churches, which cover every conceivable denomination. The larger towns also have at least one Hindu temple and one mosque, while on the predominantly Muslim coast the various branches of Islam are all represented. There is a Jewish synagogue in Nairobi.

Police

The huge numbers of police roadblocks are officially there to check vehicles, but most are actually there for the bribes. Sadly, the police force is still corrupt.

A 'white' car is rarely stopped and will never be tapped for cash. If you run into trouble, you should be treated with courtesy, but it is wiser to take someone with you as a precaution. If you are arrested, you could be in for a very rough time, so make sure that someone gets word to the embassy or a lawyer as soon as possible. As a rule, always be polite to the police and never take photographs.

Postal services

The postal system, although fairly reliable, is somewhat sluggish. It is important to remember that when sending parcels, you must take them in unwrapped for inspection by Customs. All post offices have poste restante facilities, but the pigeon-holing can be eccentric, so make sure that your correspondents write clearly and underline your surname. Post offices are open Monday to Friday, 8am to 5pm and on Saturdays, 8am to 1pm.

Public transport
Buses

There are plenty of tatty buses operating in the main cities, but relatively few long-distance ones. They are cheap, but most are very overcrowded. **Akamba Public Road**

Services is a private company offering quality shuttle services between Nairobi and Mombasa and Nairobi and Arusha (*tel: (020) 553 000. www.akambabus.com*).

Matatus

Usually either Nissan or Toyota 14-seater minibuses, these are the most common form of public transport. But they are also the vehicles most commonly involved in horrendous accidents.

Taxis

There are taxis outside the main hotels and on main streets. Negotiate a price before you get in. Taxis are not cheap.

Senior citizens

There are no special facilities or discounts for the elderly, but few tours involve a lot of walking, the facilities are comfortable and the range of food wide. The elderly should have no problems.

Student and youth travel

The YHA, YMCA and YWCA have Kenyan bases (*see p169*), but otherwise there are no special facilities or discounts for young travellers. **TST Tours**, *PO Box 50982, Nairobi (tel/fax: (020) 791 227/780 461)* specialise in technical or study tours in a wide range of fields for students and professionals on working trips.

Sustainable tourism

Thomas Cook is a strong advocate of ethical and fairly traded tourism and believes that the travel experience should be as good for the places visited as it is for the people who visit them. That's why we firmly support The Travel Foundation: a charity that develops solutions to help improve and protect holiday destinations, their environment, traditions and culture. To find out what you can do to make a positive difference to the places you travel to and the people who live there, please visit *www.thetravelfoundation.org.uk*

Telephones

The domestic and international phone systems both work efficiently and most places are on the STD network for direct dialling. Hotel charges are high. The streets of Nairobi are littered with phone boxes, but not all have phones in them yet. The international dialling code for Kenya is *254*.

Mobile (cell) phones are well established in Kenya and if you are staying for a while it would be worthwhile buying one. They cost from about US$75 upwards and all use pre-paid cards – widely available. Some useful telephone numbers are:

Operator *900*
Directory Enquiries *991*
International STD *000* or *001*
International Operator *0195* and *0196*
International Information and Call Booking *0191*

Time

The time in Kenya is GMT +3: when it is noon in Kenya, it is 9am in London,

4am in New York, 1am on the West Coast of America and 7pm in Sydney, Australia.

Tipping

There is usually a 10 per cent service charge built into hotel and restaurant bills, so tipping is an optional extra. A small amount will do for bags or other services and tipping is unnecessary in bars or taxis. At the end of a safari, leave the staff a decent tip or present.

Toilets

Toilet facilities vary. Hotels, the airports and restaurants usually have excellent facilities, but public toilets are generally to be avoided, unless you are desperate, in which case look on it as an education. Campsite toilets are usually clean and hygienic long-drops, but look out for other inhabitants – from cockroaches to bats! If camping in the bush, bury or burn your paper. Always carry some paper or tissues.

Tourist offices
Agents abroad

Kenya has abandoned walk-in offices abroad. However, it does have a good website (*www.magicalkenya.com*). Agents have been appointed in some countries. Contacts are as follows:

Canada

Discover the World (*tel: (0866/891 3909)*.

The leafy garden at Langata Link, Nairobi's 'Help You' Service

Netherlands
TMC (*tel: (020) 638 4661*).
UK
Hills Balfour (*tel: (020) 7367 0900.
www.hillsbalfoursynergy.com*).
USA
Carlson Destination Marketing Services
(*tel: (1-866) 445 3692.
www.magicalkenya.com*).

In Kenya
The **Kenya Tourist Board** is in
Nairobi (*tel: (020) 719 924/26/28/47*);
there is a totally unhelpful office in
Utali House, Utali Street, opposite
Uhuru Highway, Nairobi (*tel: (020) 331
030*), and on Moi Avenue, Mombasa
(*tel: (041) 311 231*).

Tour operators and agents
There are some 600 tour operators in
Kenya. To obtain a comprehensive list,
contact the **Kenya Association of Tour
Operators (KATO)** (*Longonot Rd,
Upper Hill (PO Box 48461), Nairobi (tel:
(020) 271 3348. www.katokenya.com*),
and the **Mombasa Tourist Association**
(*tel: (041) 225 428/311 231*).

Langata Link
This is a useful 'help you' service which
anyone in Nairobi, whether visitor or
resident, finds extremely valuable at
one time or another. The services
include: secretarial, coffee shop, travel
agent, health insurance, internet café,
etc. (*Langata South Road, Nairobi
(tel: (020) 891 314/890 480.
www.langatalink.com*).

Other useful contacts are:

**Kenya Professional Safari Guides
Association** trains safari guides and
maintains standards.
www.safariguides.com

Travel News
Travel News is the monthly east African
travel magazine, but which mostly
covers Kenya. Also by the same
publisher is the annual review *About
Kenya*, which comes out for the World
Travel Market each November. Both
contain information on what's new.
Tel: (020) 374 9637.

Travellers with disabilities
There are few special facilities for
travellers with disabilities, but there is
no shortage of goodwill. Kenyans are
generally very helpful and visitors with
disabilities will have little difficulty
getting assistance. Stick to the more
expensive hotels; facilities deteriorate
once out of the tourist zone. The public
areas and some bedrooms at most
resorts and game lodges are at ground
level, while the larger Nairobi hotels
have lifts. Few have special fittings or
wide access, however, so a travelling
wheelchair is recommended. There are
London taxis in Nairobi and Mombasa
and, with a little juggling, you can get a
wheelchair into a safari minibus. For
more information, contact the
**Association for the Physically
Disabled in Kenya**, *PO Box 46747,
Nairobi (tel: (020) 224 443*).

Index

Acknowledgements

Thomas Cook Publishing wishes to thank DAVID WATSON, to whom the copyright belongs, for the photographs in this book (except for the following images):

AA PHOTO LIBRARY 7, 9, 10, 11, 12, 13, 14, 15, 16, 17, 27, 29, 33, 40, 41, 47, 51, 55, 56, 57, 65, 66, 67, 68, 71, 84, 85, 88, 89, 90, 97, 99, 100, 102, 104, 105, 106, 112, 118, 123, 126, 127, 128, 129, 130, 140, 144, 147, 160, 167, 182 (Paul Kenward); 8, 103, 115, 151, 181 (Eric Meacher)
DREAMSTIME.COM 1 (Alex Dibrova); 38 (Paul Banton); 73 (Deborah Benbrook)
FLICKR 113 (Novecentino)
R W MOSS 91, 94
PICTURES COLOUR LIBRARY 137
SPECTRUM COLOUR LIBRARY 75, 141
WORLD PICTURES/PHOTOSHOT 21, 24, 63, 110, 135

For CAMBRIDGE PUBLISHING MANAGEMENT LTD:
Project editor: Tom Lee
Typesetter: Donna Pedley
Proofreader: Diane Teillol
Indexer: Karolin Thomas

SEND YOUR THOUGHTS TO
BOOKS@THOMASCOOK.COM

We're committed to providing the very best up-to-date information in our travel guides and constantly strive to make them as useful as they can be. You can help us to improve future editions by letting us have your feedback. If you've made a wonderful discovery on your travels that we don't already feature, if you'd like to inform us about recent changes to anything that we do include, or if you simply want to let us know your thoughts about this guidebook and how we can make it even better – we'd love to hear from you.

Send us ideas, discoveries and recommendations today and then look out for your valuable input in the next edition of this title.

Emails to the above address, or letters to the traveller guides Series Editor, Thomas Cook Publishing, PO Box 227, Coningsby Road, Peterborough PE3 8SB, UK.

Please don't forget to let us know which title your feedback refers to!